LEADING *with* LEGACY

LEADING *with* LEGACY

INSPIRED IMPACT SERIES

First Edition

Copyright © 2022 Kate Butler Books

www.katebutlerbooks.com

ISBN: 978-1-957124-44-5

Design by Melissa Williams Design
mwbookdesign.com

table of contents

INTRODUCTION

Kate Butler, CPSC

I kneel down to kiss my baby girl goodnight and whisper all the hopes and dreams and possibilities for her life into her little ear. As her mom, it is my job to breathe this belief into her. It is my job to make sure she knows she is capable of creating all she desires. And so, I whisper. She may be fast asleep, but I stay, and I continue to whisper.

"I love you, no matter what."

"You are capable of doing extraordinary things."

"Your dreams want *you* as much as you want them."

"If it's in your heart, it is there for a reason, and it is worth pursuing."

"The challenges are there to teach you what you need to know for the next dream on your path."

"There is only one *you*. You have gifts to give this world that no one else can."

That is enough for now, I reassure myself. It's only nap time. There will be more whispers of possibilities tonight. Only, I cannot get up. I cannot move. I am frozen on the ground where I was kneeling next to my baby girl's bed, where I was rubbing her back so she could fall fast asleep. I am now completely cemented to this spot.

A rush of awareness that washes over me. No one else is in the room, besides me and my sleeping baby, but I hear a voice.

Voice: "What about you?"

Me: I am frozen. *What was that?* I think to myself.

Voice: "What about your dreams? What about your unique gifts? What about your possibilities?"

Me: *Could I really be hearing this?* Everything is pouring in - the thoughts, the awareness, and what I need to know.

Voice: "What about your dreams? What about your unique gifts? What about your possibilities?"

Me: *What about me?*

Voice: "You are breathing so much belief into your children. Do you believe that for your own life?"

Me: I am flooded with agony. The awareness hits. I cannot get up because I don't want to leave the room. I don't want to walk down the steps. I don't want to walk back down to the monotony of my life for one more single moment. This is it.

Voice: "What about your dreams?"

Me: Something shifted deep inside of me. I *thought* I was living my dream. I was in love with my husband. We had two healthy children. I had a lucrative corporate job. We had just moved into what we believed would be our forever home. But in this moment, I realize this was just part of my picture, that there was more, so much more. In this moment, I begin to realize that something happened when I became a mom; I started showing up fully for everyone and everything else in my life, but I was not actually showing up for myself. I was pouring into my husband, my family, my children, my career, and my coworkers. But where in this life was I actually truly and fully showing up for *me*? Where was I dreaming? Where was I growing? Was I fulfilling my life purpose?

Voice: "You were meant for more."

Me: *I don't even know what more looks like. I don't know what my life purpose is. I don't even know where to begin.*

Voice: "How can you expect your children to believe it is all possible for their life, if you don't believe that for yourself? You have to go first."

Me: I take one long deep, deep breath.

And there it was. The last thing I needed to hear that brought everything full circle for me. That moment was the first time I can remember feeling pure, unaltered truth hit my body and then pour into me inch by inch. I felt this in every cell of my body. It felt electric, the truth of this statement vibrated through my body.

I had given up on myself. I had stuffed away my dreams. I resigned to the fact that this was life, and it was good enough. I let go of the notion that there could be more or that I wanted more. Until that moment.

I had no idea where to begin, except for the fact that I knew what I was currently doing was not working. So, I just began to ask myself, "If you do not want to continue on this path, what would you prefer?" I repeated that question to myself countless times. Every answer got me closer and closer to aligning with my soul's path.

This led me to admit to myself that deep down, I really wanted to write a book. In honoring how this all unfolded, I decided the first book should be a children's book written around breathing unwavering belief into our children. *More Than Mud* was published. The success of this book was an indication that I was clearly on the right path. So, I kept going and took one more step.

This led to our second children's book, which I co-wrote with my daughter, Bella. She became a #1 Best-selling author at five years old.

Our third book, *Believe Big*, was created by me, Bella, and Livie. Now both of my daughters have become #1 Best-selling authors before they were ten years old.

Wow, dreams really come true!

As much as the accolades were cool and, truly, a lot of fun, they were secondary to what was most important. You see, whether our books became best sellers or whether they sat on a shelf, collecting dust and failing miserably, the entire point of taking the step was to show my daughters that my dreams were worth pursuing. The point was to show them I was worth pouring into! The success or failure of these ventures was virtually irrelevant.

Regardless of how successful you are on your path, there is inevitable failure along the way, so this cannot be the measuring stick of your worth.

This was the lesson: Understanding that our dreams will always evolve; that we will always be growing into them; that win or lose, those dreams are always, always still worth going after; that you are worth taking a risk on; and that truly, no matter what, at any age, from any circumstance and from any starting point, if you have a dream, it is unwaveringly possible to fulfill.

I had to go first. It was part of my purpose to learn this lesson and walk on this path to show my children what is possible for them. In doing so, this has led to thousands of others claiming their dreams as well. This is how we make a difference: We go first. This is how we make an impact: We pursue it, win or lose, because we know the journey is what will inspire. This is how we leave a legacy: We color our path as much as possible so our gifts, our brilliance, and our imprint on the world can be seen, found, and received.

What a beautiful opportunity we each have been given. We get to live this life, create what we desire along the way, share with the world what only we can, and leave that imprint behind. Legacy is such a beautiful gift that we give ourselves—when we are creating it—and that we give others, as they get to experience it.

* * *

This book is dedicated to you. We see you, we feel you, we relate to you, and we connect with you . . . because we are you. At our core, we are more alike than we are different. We are beings of light and love who deeply desire to make a positive influence on the world with our unique type of brilliance. The pages of this book promise to fill you with the wisdom, insights, and inspiration that will align you further with your soul's path. Our hope is that the vulnerability and authenticity of these stories will remind you deeply of who you are and inspire you to claim your dreams, shine your light, and choose the legacy you leave in this world.

It is your time. It is our time. It is time.

Enjoy the unfolding . . .

ABOUT KATE BUTLER, CPSC

Kate Butler is a TV Host, Publisher, #1 International Best-selling Author and Speaker. Kate is the host of the TV Show, "Where All Things Are Possible" which streams on Roku. She is also creator of the *Inspired Impact Book Series*, a #1 International Best-selling Series that has published over 300 authors. Kate focuses on taking your story and bringing it to life in a best-selling book . . . this is her specialty!

As a CPSC, Certified Professional Success Coach, she offers dynamic live and digital programs creating transformational experiences to ultimately help clients reach their greatest potential and live out their dreams, including becoming a #1 Best-selling Author through her mentorship. Kate believes in learning the tools to help create those "Made For Moments" in your life. Her passion is teaching others how to activate their authentic mission, share it for massive impact while also creating a lucrative business.

Kate's expertise has been featured on Fox 29, GoodDay Philadelphia, HBO, PHL 17, Roku the RVN network and many more tv and radio platforms.

Kate offers a variety of free tools on her website to help you get clear on what you want and also to show you the path to make it possible. Visit www.katebutlerbooks.com

Connect with Kate:

Facebook: @katebutlerbooks
Instagram: @katebutlerbooks
Website: www.katebutlerbooks.com

SOULFUL PREGNANCY

Rosalyn Baxter-Jones, MD, MBA

Have you ever had an idea to change the way something has always been done that was so different from the norm, but you knew it was exactly what was needed?

I have. In fact, I have had my idea for the past decade!

I want to change the way expectant mothers view their pregnancies, the way healthcare providers view their patients' pregnancies, *and* I want to empower the babies while they are still in utero.

I told you it was different!

I have been a board certified, scientifically trained doctor of Obstetrics and Gynecology (OB/GYN) for the past thirty years and have always had a pull to infuse my practice with spirituality. My vision is to empower expectant mothers to embrace their pregnancy, help them conquer their vulnerability, and show them how spirituality and a life's purpose can be fulfilling. And most importantly, I want to encourage them to trust the Universe that their baby has *their* own purpose as well.

In 2009, I lost my husband, and everything shifted. My parents transitioned in 2013 and 2014. After their transitions, the questions I asked myself were,

Why am I still here?
What is my purpose in life?
What am I supposed to do now?

Not only had I lost my husband and parents, I had lost my will to live, and I was searching for guidance.

My guiding light became the messages I received and continue to receive from the Universe and Spirit.

I have always been a spiritual person, and I believe in synchronicities. I knew I needed to pay attention to what was showing up for me even though my concept for expectant mothers was so different from the way things have always been done. On a spiritual level, I knew the Universe had put me here for a reason, and what kept showing up for me was the term *Energy Medicine*. I couldn't ignore the messages any longer, so I began to explore how Energy Medicine could be used in the field of obstetrics in assisting pregnant women to help their babies grow healthy in utero. This would be especially significant with babies smaller than average size and weight. There are not many options to help underweight babies during pregnancy, but I knew in my gut I could make a difference in this space!

I also knew my vision was divergent from traditional medicine, and I was not sure how it would be received or accepted. In spite of those thoughts, I began researching how I could use Energy Medicine in my field.

My overall vision for the expectant mother is for her to see her pregnancy from a different viewpoint by encouraging her to explore the questions, "Why am I here?" and "What is my purpose?" My desire is also for her to be empowered to *know* what to do instinctively and to utilize the guidance from her midwife or OB/GYN to embrace her special journey. I want her to feel empowered and comfortable with knowing *why* she is pregnant and *why* she is bringing this child into the world, and to know and understand her child is coming into this world for a reason. I wanted to help each woman create her vision for her pregnancy outcome and what she would invite in while honoring what she is intuitively feeling.

When she goes into labor, these beliefs and practices will support her since she has been on a journey of self-empowerment throughout the pregnancy and is able to look at the experience with a totally different perspective. She will have been connecting to Spirit, the Universe, Source, and Energy Medicine and will have a better understanding with her newborn coming into the world. She will be comfortable bringing her child into the world because she feels empowered and confident. And she believes her baby has their own *why* to fulfill. I want her to view pregnancy as being empowering!

I have always been on a journey of self-empowerment. In my daily life, I embrace Spirit, Source, and the Universe to guide me. I continue to have visions of how this would look for expectant mothers—visions of how this could change the field of obstetrics by combining my medical training with the infusion of Soulful Energy. Again and again, this vision has been confirmed by several intuitives that *this* is what I am meant to be doing: embracing my vision for pregnancy of incorporating empowerment, intuitiveness, spirituality, and synchronicity.

I know for certain that using this approach will change the face of obstetrics. I am ready to be the face and the voice sharing this with the world. I keep asking myself, *Am I ready?* And the answer I keep receiving is *YES!* So, I now know with certainty *this* is my purpose.

My overall vision is to share knowledge with pregnant women in the area of self-care to empower them to be more in control of their stress and improve their pregnancy outcome. They would engage in self-care in addition to the recommendations from their healthcare providers. To be clear, I am in no way advising expectant mothers eschew information shared by their providers. What I recommend is *in addition* to what their providers guide them to do. As they incorporate the practices I share with them, these techniques will allow them to feel empowered on their own so they have the knowledge to hopefully have an improved pregnancy outcome. Many of my patients have shared how afraid they are during pregnancy, and I believe these practices will help reduce the fear that so many women face in pregnancy, labor, and delivery.

I have shared my ideas with many nurses and nurse-midwives, and they are excited to embrace this concept. I visualize overseeing a coaching program for them to learn how they can help me implement these practices with our program.

Another area of pregnancy that I am very interested in studying is following the growth of babies. I see patients who experience babies with low birth weight, and I will be requesting IRB (Institutional Institute Review Board) approval to conduct a research study assisting small babies to grow in utero. I will be studying the effect of incorporating consciousness in pregnancy. My intention is to uncover the correlation between incorporating Consciousness in Pregnancy and its impact on the babies' birth weight. With my standing in the medical community and the credentials I hold, it is extremely important for me to follow protocol in the study so my colleagues view my research with credibility and embrace the information from my findings. I anticipate the results from my research will allow me to gain clarity that will inform how best to develop my program using Energy Medicine. These programs will transform how underweight babies during pregnancy are managed during pregnancy and will be impacted with new additional tools using the protocols.

The latest information on Consciousness in Pregnancy shows that babies are conscious before, during, and after birth. Babies have visual and auditory preferences, and they also have significant awareness when born. The fetus is also able to perceive Mom's voice over a stranger's voice. Soulful Pregnancy will be able to educate Mom's on how to become more conscious and connect with their baby.

My ultimate desire is to find alternatives to always writing prescriptions, which has been the norm for decades. I am ready to create change. I am ready to disrupt the norm. In essence, I am offering a different approach to health care that I know in my gut is the path I am meant to follow. Intuitively, I feel this is so important and no longer wish to ignore the pull. I am ready to move forward with this vision. My patients deserve to know about this approach using nonlocal consciousness and energy medicine and to have the option to embrace it.

My program will include guidebooks, workbooks, and checklists that have been curated from my years of experience as an OB/GYN. It will also include recommended movement and exercises for each stage of the pregnancy, including postpartum.

I want to empower the expectant mother to question her provider—not in a way that questions their expertise, but in a way for them to view their pregnancy with a different lens. Both the mother-to-be and her doctor should know about these options. When a professional is trained in one manner, it is often challenging for them to see a different viewpoint. The professional may feel this is how we have always done it, and therefore, this is how we are going to continue to do it. But as new insights are available, and new awareness surfaces, I believe that my approach using Energy Medicine will be a welcome addition and will become more mainstream. My desire is that more scientifically trained OB/GYNs will be open to incorporating these ideas and philosophies into their practices.

I envision seeing a huge shift in this field, and I am going to be the one leading this movement. I will be on stage delivering TED Talks, leading training seminars, and building this on a much larger scale because I believe that many expectant mothers want to have this option. I imagine reducing the collective stress and fear level in pregnancy and delivery on a much larger scale. This will change the face of obstetrics! I believe this change will happen not only on a spiritual level, but it will serve to improve the outcomes of the pregnancies as well.

Why am I still here?

I know this is why I am still here and see it so much clearer now than ever before. Expectant mothers deserve to have the most positive experience possible. Pregnancy is fraught with not only changes physically but also emotionally, spiritually, and energetically throughout the pregnancy, and for many, that continues after giving birth.

What is my purpose in life?

I want to create a path for all those involved to make this experience a collaboration, a true partnership between the mother, the physician, the midwife, the patient advocate for incorporating Energy Medicine, and healers so the baby comes into the world more connected and spiritually attuned with the mother. I want to remove the fear from delivery; I want to provide space for the mother to feel confident and comfortable as she brings this precious miracle into the world. I want to change the conversation around childbirth. I want to change the experience from "I am doing what the doctor is telling me to do and not swaying from that" to "This is a partnership." Making that change will allow space for the mother to say, "What if we incorporate this piece or include this aspect into my pregnancy?" I envision the mother creating her vision for her pregnancy outcome, what she would invite in, and to honor what she is intuitively feeling.

What am I supposed to do now?

My bigger vision is to continue to be present in these mothers' lives and to incorporate these concepts of spirit and soul work with their children as they grow following the teachings of thought leaders. As women who are embracing their bodies and raising kids, *how* they are being raised under the age of seven is crucial. Dr. Bruce Lipton believes that if we can share with children the idea of consciousness, then it will change how we approach the world, how we approach making decisions, and how we approach life in general. This will be a focus of my study—combining the power of intention with the concept of Consciousness in Pregnancy and using it to shift what pregnancy, delivery, and raising children looks like.

I know there are so many of you reading this and thinking to yourself, *I so wish this was available when I was pregnant!* For many, this concept feels so natural and so aligned with those who follow Spirit as a guide, and I am honored to be the one bringing it to the forefront. Imagine the future when all babies experience a *soulful pregnancy*.

ABOUT ROSALYN BAXTER-JONES, MD, MBA

Rosalyn is a board-certified OB/GYN who has practiced obstetrics (delivering babies) for many years. During the past decade, she has realized that her true purpose in life has been to develop a special way for women to combine spirituality and consciousness to connect to their baby. She wants to provide a special environment for moms who experience fear and stress during their pregnancy. Small babies are born often without any specific reason and she is interested in trying new approaches to help these little ones in addition to traditional practice and prenatal care.

She is on a mission to encourage Consciousness in Pregnancy by educating women on what that means. Her training in integrative and holistic medicine plus functional medicine has led her to think outside of the box in educating women to empower their intuitive skills during pregnancy, delivery, and postpartum.

I MADE UP MY MIND

Dr. Lucette Beall

In December 2009, three days after my divorce was final, in which I did not ask for child support, I found out I had breast cancer as a single, self-employed mom of one beautiful, brilliant daughter. During the ensuing fifteen months of treatment that included multiple surgeries, chemotherapy, and radiation, I learned to lean on God and the Universe and completely trust that what I needed, He would provide. I finished cancer treatment in March 2011. I thought I had it down and life would be golden from then on. It's funny though how life's challenges can give you so much opportunity for incredible growth and a bigger life.

August 15, 2012, a day forever etched in my memory, my brother was injured in a freak horse accident. He was in a coma, and we were told that there was a slim chance he would make it. Both my mother and I separately felt God telling us he was going to make it. Two weeks after the accident, he began to wake up, and miracle after miracle occurred until eventually several months later, he was able to go home. While it was a miracle, he faced many challenges in the weeks, months, and years ahead.

Flash-forward to 2014. My brother had been in and out of

mental health facilities several times because the brain damage was making it hard for him to manage his temper and communicate. Almost exactly two years after his accident, I got another call. My brother had lost his temper to the extent that his wife had to call the police. My parents, in their late seventies were unable to help him, and he was in danger of having to stay in the mental hospital for the rest of his life. I felt God telling me I had to go get him. I had no idea how I could make this happen. Financially I wasn't in the place to just step out of my business, and he wasn't in a place where he could be left alone all day while I was at work. But regardless of the obstacles, the pull from God was so strong.

I had to make sure it would be safe to bring him home for me and especially for my daughter who was now seventeen. After reading, studying, talking, and planning, I felt I really could help him, and I became his guardian and brought him home to my house. I did not work in my veterinary practice for six weeks and then was only able to work one to two days a week for over a year while helping him learn coping skills and regain his independence. I was able to get him on disability and eventually move him into his own apartment while still paying his bills for him and helping him manage things.

Throughout the next couple of years, I was finding my way to get back on track.

Finally, in November 2018, I "woke up" and realized that if I wanted a better ending to my story, I had to do something about it right now. What I also realized was that it wasn't about hard work—I had been doing that for years. It wasn't about sacrifice—I hadn't taken a vacation in years either and would rarely let myself do anything other than work, grocery shop, meal prep, and get ready for the next week. No, what I realized was that I needed a change of attitude, a change of mindset. I started out knowing some of what I needed to do, and once I made up my mind and started *believing* I could change the outcome, then God began leading me down that path, step by step, action by action.

What I have come to realize is that God can only lead us when we are listening and *believing.* And believing is not just about faith, it is about attitude. The most important step I learned was that every single morning I needed to set the tone for the day. I needed to read positive affirmations, positive self-help books, pray, and meditate. At the beginning of this, I would get myself in a really great place, but then sometimes within ten minutes of getting to work, I was struggling to stay positive and not let my circumstances take me down. But with consistent work, seminars, and continuing to read, pray, and meditate every day, I began to see a shift.

When I "fell off the bike" and felt grouchy or stressed, I used coping skills to get back to feeling positive, empowered, and in control.

Then starting in late October 2019, my mother's health took a sharp decline and she began to be in and out of the hospital, and the doctors were having trouble figuring out what was wrong. My father by this point was in the later stages of dementia. He and my mother were still living alone on an almost five-hundred-acre ranch in Oklahoma. My mother did not want to leave the ranch even though it was becoming more and more difficult for her to manage my father out there alone.

As my mother's health was rapidly declining, I promised myself I would not go back to that depressed, overwhelmed state that I had allowed myself to be in while helping my brother. I was determined to continue the new path I was building for myself while helping my parents.

My mother was very independent and really struggled with the thought of needing assistance or moving. She was very headstrong, and there was no helping her until she was ready for help. For two years I knew she needed more help but had to wait until she was ready.

A few days before Christmas of 2019, after trips to the hospital in November and December, she reached out and said she thought they really needed some type of assisted living. I asked her if she would let me find a place that could accommodate both of them near me so I could help them, and she agreed to it. The miracles started to unfold again in the most amazing ways. First, I was able to find a wonderful facility in two days that could accommodate both of them and had openings—that was an incredible miracle, even more so at that time of year when many families are realizing their loved ones need help and there is usually a waiting list.

After I found the facility, the next morning, December 23, my mother had to go by ambulance again to the small-town hospital near them where they always took my dad in as well, fed him meals, provided him a bed in her room, and took him back to her room every time he got lost. As I was trying to plan with my mother on how to get them both to Texas, she had a sudden change of heart and started refusing to answer my phone calls and texts.

Not sure what to do, I contacted the lovely woman from the memory care and extended care facility, and she said, "No worries, she will change her mind again and we will be ready when she does." She agreed to hold their rooms *at no charge* while we were waiting. I debated going to Oklahoma but felt that showing up when she wasn't speaking to me, even though I had only done what she asked, might make things worse, and I so wanted to do the right thing for my mom and dad. I was unsure where to go from there.

Finally Mom reached out. We had a good conversation, she told me that she wasn't yet ready to move and that she and Dad were going to be fine, and we said our I-love-yous. After I hung up the phone, it came to me so clearly and peacefully, I don't really know how to describe it, but it was this distinct feeling: *knowing* that neither of my parents would be with me by the following Christmas. It was not scary or sad, just peaceful, but it also made me wonder, *Where did that come from and why?* Again though, I felt so much peace and love in my heart that it wasn't scary.

By Christmas Day, Mom was calling me saying she needed help and assistance and was ready for the move. We got paperwork and plans moving as fast as we could as Mom continued to struggle with her health. As we were putting plans in place, Mom and I had discussions about the fact that I (or someone) needed to be able to sign on their bank accounts so that if something happened to her, we would be able to take care of Dad. She had a hard time with that but understood and agreed that it had to be done before moving them to Texas.

I was on the way to Oklahoma to meet Mom at the bank when she called and said she was feeling really weak and terrible and didn't think she could go. I called her friend Sue to check on her. Sue called me back shortly and let me know she was taking Mom to the hospital. Luckily, Mom and Dad's longtime housekeeper/friend was there and able to stay with Dad. The banker allowed me to go to the bank and sign all of the paperwork and then take it to the hospital for Mom to sign. They were loading mom onto an ambulance to take her to Oklahoma City while she was signing the paperwork for the bank.

I went to the ranch to get Daddy and their beloved dog to take with me back to Texas so I could get him into the memory care facility where we knew he would be taken care of. The miracles here are just incredible. Daddy could not have stayed with Mom this time, as she went to the ICU in Oklahoma City. Oh, how I was thanking God for all of His guidance and all the crazy miracles that let me have the perfect place for Him at the exact moment we had to have it!

On the drive back to Texas, my Dad thought I was his sister the entire time. Only a few weeks prior while talking on the phone he had still known who I was. My sweet dad was so con-fused and lost without my mom.

Finally after ten days in ICU, we were able to get Mom moved to extended care here in Texas, which was on the same floor as my dad, but Dad was in Memory Care. The fact that they were together, in the same place, felt like a miracle.

Mom's health continued to decline, but she would prove to be determined and strong-willed right until the end, which always brings a smile to my face. Mom had emergency surgery six days after she moved to Texas. Two days later, she had the nurse call me at two a.m. to tell me she was done, she wanted to die.

The next day Mom's surgeon came by to visit her. He wanted her to let them do further diagnostics; she stuck her tongue out at him and refused. Her vital signs appeared stable, but ten minutes after he left the room, she began to crash. Mom had a DNR in place.

She went peacefully on her terms, and I was and am so grate-ful for that. I sat with Mom for a bit and just appreciated that she was at peace and no longer suffering. I thanked her for so many things, and I thanked God for letting her come home when she was ready! Mom passed away Monday, January 20, 2020.

As I sat with Mom waiting for the nurse to come to confirm her death and fill out paperwork, I realized there were a lot of things I didn't know. We both thought we had more time. But I continued to be grateful that she was at peace and that God took her home when she asked him to.

To get her affairs in order, I made a few phone calls and five of Mom's beloved friends met Michelle, my dear friend, and I at my mom and dad's house. What could have been a really difficult time was made better with dear friends, as we could share stories and memories while trying to plan and sort all the things.

Several more people came out to help, which was incredible and eased my heart so much to be surrounded by people who loved my parents (and/or me) as we sorted their things out. There were funny moments and challenging moments. A gentleman who had been my parents' friend for years, took me out on the ranch with another man in his truck and tried to get me to sign papers to auction the ranch. I was furious and refused to sign the papers. What helped me tremendously at that time was walking back into the house with so many beautiful awesome friends of my parents and me. The appreciation and love I felt for all of them plus the task at hand helped distract me from the situation that had just unfolded.

That Saturday, late in the day, I was going through some books in the guest bedroom when a female cardinal started hitting the glass window. I ran outside to see if I could distract her. She immediately flew to a tree right there next to the window and sat next to her male partner. I said, "Hello, Mom, I love you and thank you!" In that moment, I felt such peace and love and so much appreciation knowing Mom was with me. I felt so much better after that! As soon as the day was done, I called Wynona, Mother's dear friend and accountant, on the way back to Texas to tell her what had transpired. She said God (and Mom) were looking out for me that day, and she said she would help me find our best option for selling the ranch.

After Mom passed away, I talked to Dad's caregivers about the situation. Dad was so far along in his dementia that it was felt that it wasn't wise to try to explain that Mom had passed away to him because he would forget, and then when he was told again, he would have to relive that awful moment of finding out over and over again. Oh, how difficult that was. The first Sunday after she passed away, I went to visit Dad, and I lasted as long as I could, deflecting him if he asked about Mom and trying to be cheerful and funny and keep his spirits up. When I had to make a break for it, one caregiver distracted Dad, and Cynthia (caregiver) came around the corner with a big hug for me. They were all so supportive and caring not just for Dad but for me as well.

During this time, God continued to find His way in. One

day in February during lunch, I was sitting in my car talking to Wynona when suddenly a big, gorgeous, black and yellow butterfly was flying back and forth in front of my windshield—in *February* while I was sitting in the car with the heater on. I told Wynona about it and said, "Hello, Mom. Thank you for being with us today." I really felt her presence and God's, and my heart was full! That night when Wynona left work, there was a butterfly sitting on her rearview mirror. Mom made sure we both knew she was with us! Even the summer before her passing, Mom was worrying about how much she was leaving for me to do. She kept trying to sort and get rid of things, and I kept telling her, "Mom, no worries, I've got this. Just enjoy whatever time you can" (between Dad and her health). I always said she forgot that she left me Wynona, by asking Wynona to be her personal representative, and she also forgot all her dear friends that helped as well, and of course, how much God would help us all!

Wynona found, through what we could only call God Winks, a very knowledgeable company that specialized in selling ranch-type properties in multiple states including Oklahoma. The gentleman who worked for the company in our area was very, very knowledgeable and straight forward, and I felt comfortable with him immediately. He came out to the ranch, evaluated it, did his research, and went through all of it with Wynona and I so we understood exactly how he came to the valuation of the property. Then the most incredible thing happened: we got a full price offer *before* we officially put it on the market, *and* the buyer said that we just needed to remove everything we wanted and they would take care of everything else. This was huge. I was still working full-time and trying to take care of Dad. Having learned while taking care of my brother that you can't find answers when you're overwhelmed and/or feeling sorry for yourself, I just kept reminding myself to trust that God was going to handle this, and boy did He ever. Literally in one fell swoop that took so much off of my plate.

During the summer and fall, Dad's mental health continued to decline, but I was thankful that he was so well loved and cared for in memory care, especially by his sweet caregiver, Cynthia. Then the day after Thanksgiving, I got a call that Dad was being taken to the hospital and I needed to get there. When I got to the hospital, the staff sent me in the room with him. I had not been able to see him in person (except through a window or FaceTime) since March of that year. As I walked into the room, his face lit up, and he said "Lucette" with such enthusiasm and joy in his voice, it totally melted my heart. We held hands and kept saying, "I love you" to each other, and then he would doze off. A nurse came in at one point to get swabs for a COVID test and then left us alone in the room again. After I had been with Dad somewhere between forty-five minutes and an hour, that same nurse came rushing back into the room and said that Dad had COVID and I had to leave the room immediately. I was able to squeeze his hand and tell him how much I loved him before I left the room. It was the first time we had touched or seen each other in person (not through a window) in eight long months. It was the last time I saw my sweet dad.

He passed away December 11, 2020, exactly two weeks after his initial diagnosis of COVID.

While Dad was sick with COVID, I remembered that odd, calm premonition that I had on Christmas Eve of 2019. It gave me such a sense of peace. I didn't know for sure what the outcome was going to be, but I just felt that God's hand was on Dad, and either way, he was going to be okay.

The relationship I had built with God/the Universe over the last two years since that wake-up call in November 2018 graced me during that time. This didn't mean there was no pain or tears, it just meant that each time something would occur—a phone call, a card, so many things—to remind me how loved I am and how loved my dad was and that everything was going to be okay.

I thought back with awe and wonder to my mother's service

in February 2020, which had felt so much like a service for both of them. It seemed to tie into the premonition as well, and simply made me appreciate God's love and care for all of us. I came to know intimately that no matter the circumstance, God's love could carry us through all of it and provide answers and sustenance for every challenge. But we must *believe* that He can and will to be able to see the answers He showers on us when we allow it. I found that love and appreciation help me see and believe/trust in what is coming next, which allows me to feel and know the answers to the challenges.

A short time after Dad had passed away, while feeling a little stuck at work, I realized the answers that come can only be as big as what you believe. I found that for myself, I only believed *big* when it involved helping others, but I hadn't learned to believe big in God's love for me and my own worthiness of God's love. That is exactly what happened to me while and after caring for my brother that took me so low. And once I "woke up," at first, I only believed that I was worthy of not losing everything but not necessarily worthy of abundance. But even during that time period, God found a crack of belief and delivered my beautiful house in the form of a rental, and as I lived here, I grew to love and believe myself worthy of this home, and then the opportunities and solutions for me to own this house came about. Now bigger opportunities are coming my way, and life is more fun every day.

I am so very appreciative of the challenges that have taught me so much and have given me the opportunity to learn and grow and believe and love and receive and share and live in this glorious world! Thank you, God!

DR. LUCETTE BEALL

As a #1 international best-selling author/speaker, creator of Your Extraordinary Life Academy, veterinarian, and entrepreneur/business owner, Dr. Lucette Beall woke up and realized that if she wanted a better ending to her story, she had to do something about it right now! She is the president and founder of Aubrey Animal Medical Center and the creator of Your Extraordinary Life Academy. She ran her very successful animal hospital as a single parent going through cancer treatment, then while taking on the guardianship and care for her brother who suffered a traumatic brain injury, and lastly while caring for her sick and aging parents. Dr. Lucette's thirst for personal growth and seeking joy in everyday life led her down the path to become a published author.

Following her wake-up moment to build her life on her terms and not allow life circumstances or her past to dictate her future, Dr. Lucette followed her heart to become a highly sought-after speaker and launched Your Extraordinary Life Academy. She believes with all her heart that every single person is worthy of an *extraordinary* life! It doesn't matter where you came from, where you have been, or what you have done, you are worthy! Each of us was born worthy and meant to do great things. But you have to learn to believe you are worthy to step into your greatness and live a life where all things are possible!

Dr. Lucette has been featured on the TV show, *Where All Things Are Possible,* and her books include *Women Who Ignite* and *Leading with Legacy.*

Web: https://www.drlucette.net/
My free gift for you: https://www.drlucette.net/gift
Facebook: Lucette Beall

LIVE OUT LOUD

Shalini Saxena Breault

Crisis

There is so much pain and struggle in our country right now, which is simply heartbreaking. Families are struggling, children are struggling, our systems in the country are struggling . . . What *isn't* struggling?

If I could sprinkle pixie dust or wave a magic wand to take it all away, I would! There is nothing more I want to do than free people from stress, pain, and struggle.

Have you read the book, *City of Girls* by Elizabeth Gilbert? There is a line in the book that might have to be my favorite: "The world ain't straight."[1]

It surely is *not*! We are in a health crisis right now. It's not just our physical health in the form of sickness. It's become psychological. We are now experiencing a psychological pandemic.

Unfortunately, we can't control what is happening in our outer world. We can only control what is happening in our inner world. This means we can only dedicate the limited time and energy to our self-care . . . to our health and well-being. If each person did

---

1—Elizabeth Gilbert, City of Girls (New York, NY: Riverhead Books, 2019).

what they can to be physically, mentally, emotionally, and spiritually well, then we might have a shot to shift this external chaos.

We will not experience unity, harmony, or wellness in our world until we can experience it for ourselves.

We must participate in our own health and wellness as if the future depends on it because it does! There needs to be the union and integration of our body, mind, heart, and spirit (breath).

> All four!
> Not one out of four.
> Not two out of four.
> Not three out of four.
> Four out of four.
> Trust me . . . I had to learn the hard way.

Childhood Coding

I am a first-generation woman in my family to be raised in the United States of America. My parents came from India in the 1970s to pursue a dream not that many people had the privilege to pursue.

Imagine a little girl being told she is a warrior. She comes from an ancestral lineage of warriors. The little girl was fiery and had strong feelings about how she viewed life and the world that was contrary to what she was being told and experiencing. She didn't feel as though she had the power or voice to express herself fully. There were rules, expectations, and obligations that needed to be followed. Warriors are leaders, the girl believed. How then is she being asked to be a follower? She didn't feel like a warrior. Confused, misaligned messages . . . she was lost.

Conventional

I understand that I was young and maybe naïve; however, this is where I got lost in my heart. I went through life doing the "right" things.

For the first thirty-plus years of my life, I was living a pretty decent life. If you saw my life from the outside, you would think I had it pretty good.

- loving family
- wonderful friends
- good job
- married
- daughter
- social activities
- higher education
- traveling the world

It got me through thirty-plus years, but if you are not in your soul's truth or aligned in your heart, the Universe *finds* a way for you to be! The days of conformity and not listening to my heart were about to end . . .

Chaos

My life has led me in all sorts of directions that I had no intention or desire to enter . . . but the tragic event on 9/11 in 2001 changed my heart forever. My heart, as I knew it, would never be the same!

My office was in Midtown Manhattan on the East Side. But on 9/11, I was signed up for a training in our downtown office, which was across the World Trade Center.

Upon arriving to my training room, the building suddenly shook. I looked out the window to see papers—so many of them—just flying by. I was so extremely confused at this point.

Then, you heard someone running down the hall telling everyone to come to the conference room to hear the news . . . the World Trade Center was attacked.

On the TV screen, we saw fire burning in the World Trade Center . . . a big, burning hole.

Then we saw another plane on the TV screen . . . The plane

went into the other tower. Our building shook at the same time. Everyone grabbed their stuff and ran down the stairs.

I really don't remember going downstairs. There was chaos . . . confusion.

At some point I realized I was outside the building . . . across the World Trade Center . . . watching the towers burn . . . fire and smoke everywhere. It was so unreal, no one moved. We were glued watching . . . frozen in time.

I didn't know a single person. All my coworkers were back on the east side.

I felt alone, and all I could think about was my three-year-old daughter at home.

I ran back into the lobby to call my friend at the office because only internal phone lines were working at the time and I was thinking he knew all the important information needed to contact my family in case I didn't make it back to Midtown.

I was back outside in the chaos to see the towers still burning.

And then, I heard a faint voice in my ear.

Get out now!

It snapped me out of the bizarre state of mind. I automatically—very robotically—turned around and went to the subway station, which was right inside our training building.

To my surprise, there was a train already there, waiting with the doors open. I went inside.

Next stop: World Trade Center. The train didn't stop. It just kept going. Why were we not stopping for other people? The train didn't stop until we got to Midtown.

I eventually got to my office, and when I walked onto my floor, my coworkers screamed and were crying. They were happy to see me. They kept saying they didn't think I would make it. I was so confused. Why wouldn't I have made it?

What I didn't know was that after I spoke to my friend at the office and went into the subway, which was obviously at that point divinely waiting for me, in that much time (less than two minutes), the towers had come down.

I got onto the *last* train leaving downtown.

For months, I was thankful that I heard the voice and was safe.

But then an unsettling feeling began to overtake me. I kept thinking over and over again and was being haunted by these questions:

What if I didn't hear the voice? Or what if I had heard the voice and ignored it? What would my family have to say to my three-year-old girl who was waiting for me at home and needed me?

My body became a battlefield and was at war: my mind versus my heart.

I went through a life crisis. Questioning and in deep reflection about every part of my life.

How do I want to show up in the world? Was I living my best life? Was I being the best version of me? Was I in the best environment for me and my daughter?

So much internal panic and struggle. The *only* thing I knew for sure was that I was divinely pushed out to safety.

Why me? The only answer I could come up with was because there was more for me to do in this life! But I had no clue what that was.

I had a second chance to figure it out. I was committed to find the voice.

When you're given a second chance at life, you take it with everything you have, even though it is messy and seems impossible.

Three years later, I got divorced. Then two years after, I left Corporate America and New York and moved to South Jersey to be a full-time mom.

Every year on 9/11, I replay the day on 2001 as if it's happening all over again. I will forever remember that it took less than two minutes for me to act on the voice which made, in truth, the difference between life and death.

Curious

This was the beginning of my return journey to the stirrings of my heart.

Since 2006, I had done a lot of deep inner work to find my truth—to unlock my divine blueprint given by God. It's been quite the spiritual awakening. It is a dedicated path of self-study where you commit to a never-ending cycle to heal, learn, and grow. You become a student of life.

I was raised believing in the importance of health and healing. My dad is a medical doctor, so healing people has been deeply embedded in my bones.

I too wanted to heal people. The only way I thought possible was to be a Western medicine doctor. However, my brain was not wired for science. God did not give me a science-linear mind.

God has shown me the way up until now. So why would God stop now?

The healing arts found me in South Jersey. I became a Reiki Master, which is an energy healing modality based on the endocrine system. Did I mention my dad is an endocrinologist?

What I am here on Earth to do is being revealed with every step I take. I always do what I can to be aligned and part of the solution to heal people.

Clarity

The synchronicities of the last sixteen years on this journey working with the endocrine system—my dad serving medically and me serving spiritually—are not things I can or have been able to ignore.

I believe I am his daughter in this lifetime for a greater purpose so when the opportunity to obtain my PhD in metaphysical science came in 2021, I knew this was it!

Deep inner work at emotional and cellular levels has opened unimaginable paths, opportunities and possibilities for me to fully realize my divine assignment. By digging deeper, one can access higher wisdom and intelligence to guide and light the way.

My mission is to heal and restore humanity one heart at a time.

The PhD will provide an opportunity to bridge science and spirituality for optimal health and wellbeing.

I am an advocate for self-study and a holistic preventative approach to Western medicine. Integrated health and wellness are the future of Western medicine.

What I have learned in the last sixteen years on this holistic path of self-study is how to

- live in wonderment
- live in purpose
- live in passion
- live in integrity
- live in freedom
- live in empowerment
- live in constant change
- live in wholeness

This is what I want for all of you!

Change

Let's talk about butterflies. Who doesn't love butterflies?

When my transformational journey began, I was introduced to the symbolism and the life cycle analogy of butterflies. Butterflies symbolize change and transformation. The transformational life cycle of butterflies was demonstrated using the concept of life-death-rebirth.

It went something like this . . .

Life as a caterpillar, *death* in the cocoon, *rebirth* into a beautiful butterfly!

When I was introduced to see how changes in our life can

be beautiful using the butterfly as an analogy, I deeply resonated with that. I wanted to be a butterfly. Who doesn't?

What I didn't know was *life* was going to ask me to become a butterfly over and over and over again every time I said yes to change—when I said yes to more!

Your life, the people in it, the opportunities that light up your heart, the challenges that cause discomfort—all of it is for you to remember and reclaim who you were created to be.

You will be asked and required to say good-bye to old, out-dated parts of yourself in order to bloom into a better and truer version of yourself over and over.

I know it doesn't sound appealing or fun. But I promise you, it's absolutely freeing! This butterfly cycle is the self-study journey we all need to participate in and be comfortable with to unlock our divine blueprint.

This beautiful spiral always leads us back to our heart, gets us closer to our soul. With every step you take, you are saying yes to change, yes to more, yes to you!

Co-Create

The rebirth process is currently happening in our world.

As long as we are divided within our own body, as long as there is a power struggle and a constant battle between our mind and heart, there will be no unity in the outer world.

I believe the way to unity and inclusion will happen with God, our Creator! We must co-create our life with God. The energy and spirit of God is needed right now to live authentically, harmoniously, intentionally, and purposefully.

I am not referring to God in a religious manner at all. Not referring to God who is outside or separate from us. I am refer-ring to God/Spirit/Higher Power/Universe who is *in* all things. God who is living and breathing within each of us.

This is our breath. Our breath is our superpower. We have had it all along. Our breath is the God-energy within each of us.

We must understand, integrate, and embody the magnificence

and brilliance of our breath. We must use our breath to open our heart. We must then deepen the power of our breath to invite our soul essence to come forth to shine, illuminate, and radiate.

Commitment

I am passionate about sharing my story for you to see it's all possible for you too.

You are where you need to be right now. Meet yourself where you are. Be okay with where you are. Show up as you are.

You must be your own advocate and *author*ity—writer of your own story. Be the writer of your own story or else you'll be part of someone else's.

What you do for work or what role you play in your world is not who you are!

Redefine what's possible for you and your loved ones. You get to choose.

If not now, then when?

Calling

There isn't anything in the world I wouldn't do for my dad. I know he's very proud of who I am right now without the MD or PhD, but this brings the health and healing message and legacy my dad started many moons ago full circle. It won't be surprising to him though that I have to do it my way as I have always been unconventional.

I represented my dad's entrepreneurial spirit in my entrepreneur business name, Swan Goddess, LLC. He refers to my sisters and I as his Swanlets and our family home, The Pond.

It was also important for me to pass his name down, but I didn't know how. To my surprise, it was shared with me that I can include my maiden name to be part of my author name so now I write under Shalini Saxena Breault. I thought writing was the only way I could pass down the family name. God showed me another way yet again! I am now not only able to continue my dad's healing legacy with pursuing the PhD, but upon completion and receipt of my doctorate, I decided to become Dr. Shalini Saxena, PhD.

My dad is a doctor, and he came to the United States to practice Western medicine. His dream was for one of his kids to be a doctor and follow his footsteps. Unfortunately, that was not going to be fulfilled by me. God didn't give me the comprehension of medicine and practicing science in this way. God shut that piece down in my brain so I did not have the option to fall back on what I knew. I didn't have the option to go please my dad, which I would've loved to do. I didn't have the option to take the easy route because it's not why I am here.

However, what did come very naturally to me is how to connect wellness into our being. How to connect spirituality into our healing. I can do all these things innately. Others have to go back to the books and study the books that tell us what medicine is to be, what healing is, and they tell us how to do it step by step. But I already had it inside myself knowing we are natural beings of healing. We know how we can actually heal ourselves, how we can tap into the natural life force energy around us to heal.

I had to take this journey, with all the respect for science, Western medicine, and medical professionals like my dad, to have this understanding that we are here to know ourselves first before we hear from someone else telling us what to do when it comes to our well-being.

I had to go through my spiritual awakening and self-study, and now as I am in this position of self-mastery, I understand I am here to bring healing and wellness in a bigger way. So, when God put the PhD program in my lap, I knew this was it and said yes! The PhD is the bridge. This is how everything connects. I couldn't just go and get my PhD before I got to this point in my own self-mastery because I was not ready to bridge the two things together.

Now I can understand how there is a place for everything. Now, I can build this dream for my family, but I am doing it in a way that honors me. I am doing it in a way that honors my path.

We all have the opportunity to do this for ourselves. I deeply believe that part of my soul mission here is to show everyone . . .

1. You have to follow your path.

2. You have to know yourself.

3. There is an option for self-mastery.

4. This is the future of wellness.

Part of my mission here on Earth in this time and space is to also show people that this exists and is available to everyone.

We are here to build our empire . . . our legacy.

We are here to live out loud!

Let's go!

The health of our world is as good as the health of its people.

ABOUT SHALINI SAXENA BREAULT

Shalini is the Creator of Swan Goddess, LLC. She is a soul healer, corporate wellness consultant, #1 award-winning and best-selling author, speaker, and the future Dr. Shalini Saxena, PhD. She is a visionary and is dedicated to a holistic approach to health and wellness. You can experience all the knowledge and wisdom she learned and integrated for yourself through a variety of ways:

Course: Shalini's Signature Online Course, Restoreth the Breath, is a guided, self-study course that teaches you to master inner stillness in the midst of external chaos, confusion, or overwhelm. You can find more information at https://www.restoreththebreath.com/. **Coaching:** Shalini provides a six-week Reiki coaching program for self-healing and healing others as a business. **Corporate:** Shalini offers chair yoga, meditation, and vision board goal-setting sessions for corporate wellness, school events, and group events. **Children:** She offers author visits for her children's books, *Hello Sun Moon and Stars* (available in English, Spanish, French, and Greek); and *Do You Believe in Angels? Angel Winks and Whispers.*

Website: www.swangoddess.com
Amazon: www.amazon.com/author/shalinisaxenabreault
Etsy: www.etsy.com/shop/MantraMalasbyShalini
Facebook: Swan Goddess
Instagram: @shalini.saxena.breault
LinkedIn: Shalini Breault
YouTube: Shalini Saxena Breault

To receive your free Bring Calm and Order to Your Inner Chaos chart, visit Shalini's website today and learn simple yet powerful healing techniques for mental, emotional, and self-esteem distress.

I KEEP SURPRISING MYSELF!

Donna Nudel Brown

Have you ever experienced that feeling when you know you are in the exact right place? Where you have found your people, your tribe, your cheering section, your supporters, and the ones who hold the place for you to step into the best version of yourself?

I have and still have moments of disbelief of where I am!

I question my place in the world.

I question the impact I have made.

I question the legacy I am creating and will leave behind.

I question it even after all I have achieved.

I am surprised by the woman I have become . . .

I am surprised by all the lives I have touched, how others see me, all that I have accomplished, and the accolades I have received and continue to receive.

I look at the women who surround me, who include me, who seek my viewpoint, and who view *me* as their peer. They graciously offer me a seat at their table. I see *them* as incredibly successful women. I often want to pinch myself to ensure all these experiences are real and authentic. Hearing how others see me continues to amaze me and I am *slowly* allowing myself to feel as though I belong.

I keep surprising myself!

The stories you are reading; the authors of these chapters are women I have looked up to, admired, and—in true transparency—have at times been a bit intimidated by because of their visibility, their accomplishments, their stature, their confidence, and their place in the world.

My journey to this point was a long and winding road, and the catalyst that led me to sharing my story with you began on the coast of New England in August of 2014 during our annual family vacation. That day changed the course of my life and continues to have a profound impact on my life.

You see, there was a long period of time when I had trouble finding my smile, finding my joy, and didn't think it was possible. I had been living with regret, self-doubt, low self-esteem, overwhelming feelings of not belonging, and I had no idea who I was outside of being a mom. I loved being a mom to my three children (now twenty-seven, twenty-five, and twenty-one) and totally hid behind that role because I had no idea who I was without that title.

I left college before graduating, and that decision left me feeling like a failure. I saw myself as not being smart. That view of myself kept me playing small for over thirty years! I hid, didn't participate in conversations, said no to most things, and I am certain during that time I never wore a smile like you see in the photo on the next page.

In August 2014 while on a family vacation, my children were cliff jumping and asked me to join. I declined and played photographer for nearly two hours capturing all their thrills and fun. My daughter repeatedly asked me to join, and I continuously said no. As the window of opportunity was closing (the tide was going out and would no longer be safe), I realized if I left without jumping, I would go on to regret it and did not want one more regret in my life!

I made my way to the top of the cliff, took a deep breath, and through total fear, I leaped! I pushed off the sandy bottom and came out of the water with my fist in the air, screaming, "I DID IT!" It was the most exhilarating feeling I can remember experiencing aside from jumping from a plane at nineteen during a time in my life when I was fearless!

That leap completely changed my life and I began to see myself as brave and confident!

As the Universe would have it, I was scheduled to attend a one-day workshop upon my return from that trip where I met my first coach—Kate Butler, the publisher of this book. That encounter opened new doors for me as I spent a year working on myself, my beliefs, and my mindset, and I learned how to dream again. I attended more events, I focused on uncovering who I was and my true desires, rediscovered my bravery, and began to say yes to any and every opportunity I was drawn to including writing a chapter in collaborative books, *Women Who Ignite* in 2016 and *Women Who Rise* and *Permission Granted* in 2020.

I keep surprising myself!

Each time someone asks me how I knew what I wanted to do (I actually had no idea!) or how on earth I found the courage to leap from that cliff, I return to the memory of that day and vividly recall the moment I decided I could not sit with my regret one moment longer. I had declined to jump for over two hours until I finally said yes and made my way to the top of the cliff.

As I was standing with my toes dangling over the edge, shaking with fear, my husband yelled, "It's now or never!" For a moment, as I was standing on that edge, I considered backing away. And then I remembered what had brought me to this point after saying no for so long. *Regret*. Regret to saying no to people, no to events, and no to opportunities. No to showing up for others or situations that intimidated me. No to speaking my truths out of fear of what others would think of me.

In that moment, I realized I had a very small window where the Universe aligned these perfect conditions allowing me this opportunity for me to literally *leap* into my future. I realized I was going to take that leap, or I was going to stay in that space forever. With that thought, I took one last deep breath, and I chose my future!

If I had allowed that moment to pass me by, my life would not look like it does today. I most definitely would not be sharing my story with you today, and I know with certainty, I would still be hiding in plain sight.

I keep surprising myself!

We each have those moments when the cliff appears and we must decide whether or not to leap. It may be a physical cliff similar to my experience or any difficult choice you are walking toward or away from—including a person, a thing, an event, or a situation that requires deep, personal introspection.

In that moment of fear and uncertainty, I decided to take the leap that would allow me to leave all my regrets behind.

I leaped and came out of the water a completely different person! Everything had shifted! My husband looked at me as if to say, "Who are you?!"

I had been so stuck where I was in my feelings of regret and self-doubt.

Stuck in what I thought was what I deserved for all the poor choices I had made in my life.

Stuck with my inner voice telling me I wasn't good enough or worthy of joy.

What I learned is that one of the best ways to get unstuck is to move your body! Emotion is energy *in* motion. If you do not like where you are or what you are feeling, *move your body*! When you change the motion of your body, your emotions will follow.

I had definitely moved my body, and I was now in a completely different place!

When I got out of the water that day, I felt the unwavering confidence and courage that I had longed for my entire life, that allowed me to say yes to new opportunities—to any opportunity I was drawn to! It led me to believe in myself and my abilities to impact others. It provided me the ability to say yes, the power to follow my intuition, and the *knowing* that I was on the right path.

I keep surprising myself!

I lived my entire adult life listening to my inner critic and believed the story I told myself that I was not smart. That story impacted my life on such a profound level. Thirty years after graduating, I learned many of my classmates thought I was one of the smartest people they knew! To this day, I recall that conversation and still shake my head in disbelief.

What stories are you telling yourself?

Once I released that belief of not being smart, it led me to believe in myself and created the space for me to say yes to new opportunities. I peeled back many, many layers to find my true self, which has allowed me to fully live an authentic life. I have found my voice and choose to share my truths and lessons with others without fear of judgment. I am proud of myself and all that I have achieved.

I am so grateful to have the ability to guide others because I myself have been through a transformational journey. I know what it is like to feel as though you do not know your purpose, to feel as though you do not belong, or to live your life just going through the motions. I felt that way until I no longer could, which led me to step way out of my comfort zone! Through total fear, I leaped off that cliff, allowing me the space to step into a new life. I found belief in myself, I found confidence in myself. I found my joy! It was as though my life went from being in black and white to beautiful, bright, vibrant colors!

I now have the desire, the ability, and the confidence to say yes to new things, to new opportunities, to continue to grow and learn, and to keep stretching. I do not want anyone else to stay in the space of unworthiness, self-doubt, and regret any longer—I have been there and know what it is like to be on the other side of that.

I keep surprising myself!

I now regularly receive invitations to collaborate and to share my story in others' communities. I was invited to be the featured resident in a local digital magazine as well as a local print magazine, which included my photo on the cover and an article of my journey. I now know I am totally worthy of receiving the accolades, the recognition, and all the love I receive.

I honestly believe this is only the beginning of my journey. You see, we are never there! There is always space to grow, to learn, to explore more adventures, and to open our hearts and minds to receive more. There are most definitely more leaps in my future!

Your leap can be anything you are walking toward or away from. It can be embarking on a new adventure, starting or exiting a job, moving across town or across the country. It can be a decision to start a family. It can be a reconciliation of or the decision to leave a relationship. We are all faced with difficult decisions in our lives; the key is to listen to your body for the answers and follow your intuition.

Did I see any of this myself? Absolutely not—not one tiny bit! It took a great deal of convincing for me to share the first part of my story in 2016 in *Women Who Ignite*. I held the intention that if I could inspire just one person, the fear of sharing my story would be worth the discomfort. Within weeks of its publication, I was contacted by a woman who read my story and wanted me to coach her. And here I am, several books later, sharing my continued transformation and guiding others through theirs.

I keep surprising myself!

That leap has allowed me to surround myself with women I never would have approached because of my lack of confidence. I now share space with these women. I recently shared the stage with many of these women—my beautiful co-authors in this book!

I keep surprising myself!

What I learned on this journey after taking that leap in 2014 is, we all have a story. We all can make an impact when we say yes to ourselves, follow our gut, and take that leap. We all have the opportunity for transformation and to make an impact if we are open to it! That cliff appears as anything we are walking toward or away from, and we take that leap when the pain of staying where we are is greater than the fear!

I honestly believe this is only the beginning of my journey. You see, we are never there! There is always space to grow, to learn, to explore more adventures, and to open our hearts wider.

I believe in myself and my dreams, I have confidence now and the belief I can do anything. I am beyond grateful to have an amazing marriage and loving relationship with my husband who supports me while I follow my dreams. I am incredibly grateful for the ability to focus on my passions now that my children are grown. And *most* importantly, I now feel more in alignment with who I am at my core and am finally living a truly authentic life!

I keep surprising myself!

I now confidently believe that anything and everything is possible. If you are thinking that I was lucky or that it could never happen to *you*, I totally understand. I felt that way as well until I learned the power of our thoughts, the power of our intention, and the power and necessity of doing the deep, personal work. Only then did I see how truly powerful I was!

You have that ability as well.

Think to yourself: when are the moments in your life where you leaped and where you didn't?

When in life were you faced with a decision of staying where you were or doing something uncomfortable? Perhaps it was standing in a doorway deciding whether to enter, or picking up the phone to resolve a conflict, or having a difficult conversation knowing you would feel deep pain. Now is the time to finally decide to make yourself a priority and evaluate all areas of your life including your health, your relationships, your career, your financial situation, your joy, and deciding *you are worthy* of having abundance in all areas of your life!

Everyone has their own cliff. Everyone needs to take a leap.

That cliff appears when the pain of staying where you are is greater than the fear of taking the leap.

What moment will *you* choose?

I encourage you to step up to the edge, take a deep breath, and leap into your future!

We *all* deserve joy!

Are you ready to say yes to yourself, to find yours?

It is never too late!

It's time to surprise *yourself!*

ABOUT DONNA NUDEL BROWN

Donna is an intuitive energy coach, Reiki Master and teacher, inspiring speaker, crystal expert, and #1 international best-selling author. Donna guides women who have put their own dreams on the back burner while taking care of everyone else and are now ready to focus on themselves. Together they dust off their dreams, align them with who they are currently, uncover and discover what the next chapter looks like, and create the path to fulfillment and joy. She often supports empty nesters as she knows the space quite well.

Incorporating Reiki and crystals in her practice, Donna's clients often experience clarity, focus, insight, and a sense of calm. Donna is grateful for her ability to support and guide others on their journey and is especially grateful she is able to do so remotely.

Using her pendulum, Donna selects the exact right crystals for her clients. Her pendulum also assists them in seeking answers to life's tough questions, allowing them to follow their path to find joy.

Donna is excited to see how her life will continue to unfold and evolve in the most amazing way. She is open to any and all possibilities and continues to say yes to all that aligns with her vision, her passion, and her purpose.

www.DonnaBrownDesigns.com
Donna@DonnaBrownDesigns.com
Instagram: @crystals_to_clarity
FB group: Leap Into Fabulous
LinkedIn: Donna Nudel Brown
Linktr.ee: Donna.Brown.Designs

FINDING THE LIGHT THROUGH THE DARKNESS

Ellen M. Craine

"Even in darkness it is possible to create light."

—Elie Wiesel

We all have a light that shines bright within us. Sometimes, the perceived darkness of the challenges we face seems to get in the way. A loss happens and we experience a grief reaction. The loss could be a seemingly everyday event, like our child graduating from kindergarten and going in to first grade. It could be more traumatic like a death or the diagnosis of an illness or a divorce/relationship ending. And it could be something in between. Regardless of the identified loss, these are life transitions that we must learn to navigate in a way that is healthy and empowering. What that looks like for each of us will be different based on our life experiences, current coping skills, and ability to add to our coping skills toolbox. Our past influences our present, which in turn influences our future.

What is important to keep in mind is that with all of these life transitions, there is always some kind of grief reaction. A grief reaction is any number of emotions that we feel around the perceived or actual loss. These feelings can range from sadness, to anger, to bargaining (where we wonder what we could have done differently), to denial, to acceptance and many other feelings as well. We go through these emotions in a way that is logical for who we are and what our life experiences have given us. Some of us seem to move through these feelings effortlessly and others struggle to make it from one day to the next. All of this is normal. In society, there is too much silence around loss and grief and too many expectations that it is something to "just get over." For many people, loss represents darkness, and finding the way through represents light. Learning how to navigate these transitions in our life is one principle to living through loss and grief.

Connecting with nature and seasonal celebrations is one way to help guide us through these perceived dark times and learn to navigate through these transitions in life. I might even argue that these life transitions are necessary since they have the power to help us grow and evolve to a higher level of consciousness if we do not stay stuck in a cycle of anger, bargaining, and sadness, which I see all too often in people I work with. These challenges can help us become more of who we are meant to be in this lifetime if we listen to the lessons the universe is giving to us. We may not always be able to grasp the lesson right away or be able to make sense that a lesson is possible, especially with a death or the diagnosis of a serious illness. However, I can promise you that there are lessons to be learned if we open ourselves up to receiving them.

Nature and seasonal celebrations provide us with a guide that let us know that even in darkness, there is light. The autumn equinox is one example where this time can be used to prepare for shorter periods of light and increasing darkness to our days. Some people use this as an opportunity to pull more inward in reflection and soul searching. Journaling and walks in nature are great activities to participate in to facilitate this process. The idea is that when we connect with the universe through nature, we are open to receiving all gifts and miracles the universe has in store for us. Perhaps most important is that we have to *want* to receive these gifts and set the intention to do so.

Another seasonal celebration that stands out is Michaelmas. Michaelmas occurs in the late fall just before the darkest and coldest days of winter arrive. During Michaelmas celebrations, a dragon represents our own human challenges. The dragon gets slain representing the inner courage it takes to find and bring forth our own inner light and growth that we must find as the growth from the earth and the sun and the warmth are fading. A spiral of light is created with evergreen branches and glowing lights or candles that people can walk through to find their own courage to bring out their inner light to help get them through these upcoming days. It definitely takes courage to bring out our own inner light, especially when we are suffering and in a perceived dark or challenging place regardless of the cause.

A couple of other holidays and seasonal celebrations that relate to finding the light through the darkness include the Jewish holiday of Yom Kippur and the Hindu festival of Diwali. Yom Kippur is the holiest day of the year for the Jewish people and has atonement and repentance as its central themes. Atonement is facilitated through prayer and fasting. During this holiday, the soul is said to be absolved of "mistakes" from the year before. Repentance is sought through prayer, community service, and asking others and oneself for forgiveness. Through these activities, there is a healing of the soul. According to Jewish oral tradition, the soul is also known as wind, spirit, living one, and unique one. Through fasting, the body is made to feel uncomfortable. I have fasted; it is true!

The soul is considered to be the life force in the body. When we make our body uncomfortable, one's soul is said to be uncomfortable. This is intended to teach us empathy. By feeling our own pain, we can have empathy for others and their pain. This is akin to walking in the shoes of another though no pair of shoes fits two people exactly the same way. Pain is an aspect of grief from life transitions or losses. It is necessary for us to grow and evolve in our consciousness and connection to the universe and each other.

Diwali is a Hindu festival of lights, celebrated in autumn in the northern hemisphere and in spring in the southern hemisphere. This festival symbolizes the spiritual "victory of light over darkness, good over evil, and knowledge over ignorance." During Diwali, there are feasts, and people light fireworks, clean and repair their homes, wear their finest clothes, and light up the inside and outside of their homes. It is so fascinating to see yet another festival that addresses the issue of finding light through the darkness.

As I come to terms with the perceived darkness in my own life, I am comforted by the teachings of the universe through these and other holidays and festivals. This is a universal theme that applies to all people. There really is more that unites us rather than divides us. Perceptions of darkness in the day-to-day human sense comes from many sources: trauma related to COVID-19, environmental/weather crises, and the impact of these on our economy, politics, and spiritual and physical well-being. Some of us have experienced, or are experiencing, more personal traumas. None of these things we can control totally on our own. What we can control is how we respond to them. This, in turn, gives us power over them and allows us to be open to receiving gifts from the universe to take away from these experiences.

There have been fourteen years of episodes of darkness in my life. Fourteen years ago, my mother died at age sixty-six from early onset dementia, most likely Lewy body dementia. She began showing symptoms around the age of fifty-eight and was officially diagnosed at the age of sixty. There were many challenges during that time and after my mother's death. It is crazy to think about it all now as I just turned sixty. Thankfully, my brain seems to be in one piece, though my children (age nineteen and twenty-two) question that at times.

Eight years ago, May 14, 2014, the next major challenge or life transition occurred when my now nineteen-year-old was diagnosed at the age of eleven with pediatric cancer. We spent four months in out of the hospital while he received intensive chemotherapy. My family grew to include the nurses and doctors that cared for us daily. I needed to work hard to get any sense of self-care into my life. My husband took care of our other son. I am grateful to be able to share that Michael is now an eight-year survivor. We maintain our relationships with his medical team. I developed a passion to give back to them and other pediatric patients and families any way I could. We set up a fund to support families receiving integrative medicine consultations for those who cannot afford it and want it. In addition, we recently completed a children's book drive and delivered well over 100 books donated by authors of children's books and other people as well. Community service is one takeaway from all the heartache we endured from this experience. I gained such a level of empathy for other families in similar and worst-case scenarios that I knew I had to step up and help in some way. There is a saying, especially with pediatric cancer, that people like to bury their head in the sand and pretend it does not exist or could not happen to them, and then it does. It totally changes one's perspective on life and what we take from the universe when these challenges are put before us.

Two years later, April 26, 2016, my husband, Marty, very unexpectedly died from a brain tumor (Stage IV inoperable glioblastoma) at the age of fifty-eight, just six weeks after diagnosis. When I wrote about this in *Women Who Dream*, the ninth book in The Impact Book series, I wrote that I was not totally sure what "lessons" or "gifts" were to come from this. Reflecting on it now, I can see that while I miss my husband every day, there has been a spiritual opening to the universe that might not have happened in the same way were it not for his passing. I will always be grateful to Marty for his unconditional love and support and for gifting me with our two amazing sons. His death also provides gifts that help get me through the dark days of missing him and what he is not physically here to witness. I do believe that his spirit is here and he is cheering Michael, Matthew, and I on.

Three years later, in the summer of 2019, my dad was diagnosed with pancreatic and bladder cancer. I became a caregiver, again. He had two years of doing well, then in the fall of 2021, a spot showed up on his lung that turned out to be a remnant from his pancreatic cancer. It was treated, and so far, he is doing pretty well for an eighty-five-year-old man. I realized I have learned so much about navigating the cancer world and advocating for medical care for others that I can help support people on their journey.

Another life transition happened in October 2020 when our family dog was diagnosed with a tumor in her belly and she had to be put down. It was a very difficult time. Shayna was my support animal, even sleeping in my bed on my husband's pillow. The day after Shayna died, I found a lump in my left breast. I could not believe it. I was petrified and kept trying to tell myself it was nothing. A few days later, I called my doctor and got in for an exam. I had just seen her in July and everything was fine. In November, I was diagnosed with Stage II breast cancer. As it turns out, my dad and I share a genetic mutation that predisposes us to certain types of cancer. I completed eighteen rounds of chemotherapy and had a double mastectomy. I am now considered cancer free and a "survivor."

Some people have asked me how I am still standing. I am still standing because I love life and trust that the universe still wants me here on this earth in my human form to receive more gifts and to be able to share my gifts with the world. This is not to say that I do not feel challenged at times, because I definitely do. I try every day to incorporate self-care into my routine: healthy eating, adequate sleep and hydration, exercise, and gardening, to name a few. With each challenge, I have come away with gifts that guide me to share with others and support them on their lifelong journey through life's transitions I call living through loss and grief. In doing so, my light continues to shine and does so in ways I could only imagine.

According to the Cambridge dictionary, the word *legacy* can be defined as "something that is a result of events in the past." The events in my life have definitely facilitated me in creating my legacy. And this process will continue as long as I am alive. This chapter, and my message in it of "finding light in the darkness" is part of my legacy in my lifetime. It is a legacy I give to my two sons, Matthew and Michael. Without their grounding force in my life, I would be struggling to find my own light and let it shine. I want them to know that no matter the hardships they face, they have a light inside of them that shines and can help them through the darkness if they let it. It is a legacy for the universe and the people who will feel touched, called, inspired, and empowered to search for and allow their own light to shine.

In my program, Living Through Loss and Grief, I guide you through the principles outlined in this chapter: navigating through transitions including how to fill your cup and have better self-care. By embarking on this journey, your light can rise up through the darkness, and it can be your guide. We all have this light within us, even in the darkest of times.

"People are like stained glass windows. They sparkle and shine when the sun is out, but when the darkness sets in, their true beauty is revealed only if there is a light from within."

—Elizabeth Kubler-Ross

ABOUT ELLEN M. CRAINE

Ellen M. Craine is in private practice as a licensed clinical and macro social worker in the state of Michigan. She owns Craine Counseling and Consulting Group and has over twenty-five years of experience working with couples, families, groups, and individuals in a variety of capacities. Ellen M. Craine is an effective trainer and educator. She teaches a variety of continuing education classes around ethics for social workers, including informed consent and telehealth, subpoenas, loss and grief, custody and co-parenting issues, and success principles for social workers and others. You can see a full list of her offerings and upcoming events on her website at www.crainecounseling.com.

Ellen M. Craine had her master's degree in social work from the University of Michigan. In addition, she has a certificate from the Institute of Integrative Nutrition in Health Coaching and is a certified trainer in Jack Canfield's Success Principles. Ellen M. Craine is a #1 International Bestselling Author in *Women Who Empower*, the seventh book in the Impact Book Series with Kate Butler. Ellen M. Craine is a co-associate producer of the documentary, Authentic *Conversations: Deep Talk with the Masters*. This documentary is the first in the documentary series and is written, directed, and produced by LA Emmy nominated Dr. Angela Sadler Williamson.

You can learn more about Ellen M. Craine and reach out to her to schedule one of her workshops/trainings or individual or group work on her website:

www.crainecounseling.com
Facebook group: Living Through Loss and Grief
Facebook page: Craine Counseling and Consulting Group
LinkedIn: Ellen Craine
Email: ellen@crainecounseling.com

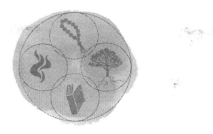

THE BRANCHES YOU LEAVE BEHIND

Ann Marie Esparza-Smith, M.A.

There's an old Japanese legend that tells us that many thousands of years ago in the central part of Japan, there was a mountain with a flat top surrounded by dense jungle. And as the legend goes, this mountain was called "the place where you leave your parents." And if one's parents reached a certain age, their children carried them through the jungle up to the top of this mountain and left them there for the gods. One day, a strapping young man fights his way through this dense underbrush, heading for the mountain and carrying a wisp of an old lady. As he fought and pushed to kick the brush aside, always heading for the mountain, he noticed that she was doing something with her hand. Finally, he turned and looked up at her, half angry at what he was doing and half angry at her, and he said, "Mother, what are you doing?" And the old lady looked down at her son, tears streaming down her wrinkled cheeks, her eyes filled only with love for her boy as she said, "Son, I'm just breaking off a few branches and dropping them to mark a path so after you leave me, you'll be able to find your way back home."[1]

1—*Og Mandino*, Gateway to Success and Happiness, audiobook (Manhattan, New York City: BN Publishing, 2019).

To leave "branches" so you can find your way back home, what does that mean? It could mean different things to different people, but for me, I believe that whether you are a parent or a parent figure, we are blessed to be able to leave "branches" for those that follow. That could be our children, our family, our friends, or those we are blessed to cross paths with.

Whether we realize it or not, someone is always watching what we do, how we handle situations, how we respond to circumstances. This is especially true with our children. Without even realizing it, how we act, respond, react, and live our lives are all branches. The way we love is a branch. The way we treat people, especially those who society casts to the side, are branches. The kindness we show to everyone is a branch. The values we live are branches. The way we celebrate is a branch. The list goes on and on.

The mother in this story left branches for her son so he could find his way back home. This resonated with me so deeply recently on two occasions. First, my bonus daughter just got married a few weeks ago. As we were planning her wedding and preparing for her special day, I wanted her day to be magical. I wanted her to feel as beautiful as I see her. My husband and I spared no expense in giving her a wedding fit for a princess. While I didn't raise her, I spent the last few years leaving her branches of love, support, understanding, kindness, and guidance so that after she leaves, she can find her way back home. I wanted to create a place at home where she wants to be. Where her and her new husband want to pop in for dinner or just to say hello. You see, the branches I leave lead to a safe, happy, fun place we all call home. The branches I left for her were designed to let her grow and be independent, strong, God-guided, and confident so she would go out and create a fabulous life for herself. I wanted her to learn what branches she would develop so that when she is a mother, an aunt, a leader in her own profession, she would leave branches that others want to follow or figuratively come home to.

The second was my kids. My son is a high school senior. As he starts his last year of high school, I reflect on how fast the time has flown. Did I prepare him with everything he needs? Does he believe he is enough, even though we tell him he is? Will he use the branches we specifically picked for him? Will those branches strengthen his moral compass so he always finds his way home? And then there is my daughter. She is a college freshman. Moving my daughter into her college dorm, what a thrill and heart wrencher at the same time. It hit me like a ton of bricks that she was leaving for college, that she was an adult moving on to her next chapter of life. Did I teach her everything she needed to know? Did I model a great life that she wanted to imitate? Did I leave enough branches? Were they good branches? Were they branches that one day both my kids would leave for their children? The reality of this moment for me was that the branches we leave are really a legacy. For me, my legacy, my wish, is that when I die, the branches I put down every day of my life make this world a better place. That the branches I left made my kids better people. People that make a difference in this world.

I believe that each of us are born with an internal moral compass, the ability to judge what is right and wrong and act accordingly. We innately know what feels good and what doesn't. In a healthy environment, that internal compass is strengthened by setting shared expectations, developing and modeling good behavior, teaching values and integrity, and surrounding ourselves and our families with people who share our same values and moral beliefs. But what if we didn't come from a healthy environment? What if there were no branches left for us? What if the branches left for us led us down a troublesome path?

The Power of Positivity wrote, "You can't change the past. So, settle your mind, let go, relax and create a better future."[2] The beauty of life is that we have the power to create a life we want,

---

2—Power of Positivity (website), accessed September 22, 2022, https://www.powerofpositivity.com.

despite our past. Perhaps you were raised in an environment where drugs and alcohol were abused. This led to your basic needs not being met. You didn't grow up in an environment that nourished your physical and emotional well-being. But you don't have to continue the cycle. You have the power to break the cycle and create a life that you want. "But how?" you may ask. "How do I let go of the branches that don't serve me and get new branches?"

There are thousands of books from people who broke cycles and created a life of their dreams. Oprah Winfrey is an excellent example of someone who wanted and desired better. I'm certain that she was left many branches that she chose not to follow—and some that she did. But all of her experiences and her choices led her to finding new branches that she would leave for those who would follow in her steps. For me, I chose to seek out people who had a life I wanted. I read numerous books on family, kindness, wealth, spirituality. All the areas that I wanted to learn and grow in, I found answers in books.

One author was Jack Canfield, creator of Chicken Soup for the Soul book series. I have read every book he wrote. I once saw him in the film, "The Secret,"[3] and he said, "My life has truly become magical. I think the kind of life that everybody dreams of is one I live on a day-to-day basis. I live in a four-and-a-half-million-dollar mansion. I have a wife to die for. I get to vacation in all the fabulous spots of the world." Those words just impacted me like no others. I wanted those branches!

So I borrowed his words and made them my own. I began to say, "I live in a four-and-a-half-million-dollar home. I have a husband to die for. I have crazy amazing children. We travel to the most fabulous places in the world." These words were now part of my "branch language."

In 2015, sitting on a fabulous beach in New Zealand, I turned to my family, with tears running down my face and said, "I live

---

3—*The Secret*, directed by Drew Hariot (Prime Time Productions, 2006), Prime Video.

in a multimillion-dollar home. I have a husband to die for. I have crazy amazing kids. We are in one of the most fabulous places in the world." I followed Jack Canfield's branches and created new ones for me and my family. All the hours I spent reading and applying what people did who had a life I wanted for myself paid off. The funny part of this whole thing is that these mentors of mine have no idea that the branches they left would guide me to an incredible life, an incredible home.

In 2017, I met Jack Canfield. To say he is one of the most amazing people I have ever met is an understatement. I had the opportunity to thank him for being my "secret" mentor and literally guiding me to transform my life into a dream life. I am so proud to have him as one of my friends, and I will always cherish the branches he left me, branches that I proudly have added to my legacy.

So you see, we may not have been left a good path of branches, but we have the privilege of seeking new branches, ones that lead us to the life we want. In the big picture, we all have the opportunity to create the life of our dreams. And if we were blessed with good branches, yay! But don't stop there. Add to your branches. Look for ways to make things better. Improve your branches. Be kinder, be more generous, be more compassionate, be a better version of you.

Remember, our branches are our legacy. Someone is always watching what we do, how we handle situations, how we respond to circumstances. This is especially true with our children. Without even realizing it, how we act, respond, react, and live our lives are all branches. So act better. Respond with kindness. React in a way that is loving. Love better, treat people with more mercy. Forgive. Live a life of integrity. Live a life that makes a difference. Be grateful. Laugh often. And celebrate every day.

When we get to that mountain at the end of our life, I want us all to look back and see all the branches we left. I want all of our children to find their way back home to their true self, to the place where they live their best life. The place where dreams come true. The place where they live with a desire to make a difference. I want the branches we leave to make each generation better than the last.

ABOUT ANN MARIE ESPARZA-SMITH, M.A.

Passionate about creating a life of her dreams, Ann Marie Smith has spent years researching the blueprints of success. She knew there was more to life than just existing. She knew that with the right tools she could learn to intentionally create a life that would matter and make a difference in the world, and with an abundance of financial resources, she could serve the needs of others as well as her own.

Ann Marie is an award-wining professional and entrepreneur. In 2019, she became an international best-selling author. She has landed coverage in print and broadcast outlets around the world, including the Univision, Telemundo, CBS, NBC, ABC, iHeart radio, and most recently Success Today. In addition to her extensive background in education and business, she most recently earned her California Contractor's License to pursue her goal of building custom homes for at-risk members of her community. Ann Marie holds a master's degree in human development/educational leadership and social change.

Ann Marie lives in Southern California with her husband and two children. In her spare time, she loves spending time with her friends and family. She believes the key to her success is prayer, gratitude, kindness, and making everything she does fun.

MY GIFT TO HUMANITY

Claudia Fernandez-Niedzielski

Legacy comes from the Latin verb *legare,* "to appoint by a last will, send as an ambassador." Originally, the noun meant "ambassador" or "envoy" but soon shifted to mean the money and property a person leaves behind in his will.

I want to stick with the original meaning of "to appoint by last will, send as an ambassador" because I believe that is what we truly are. Ambassadors of our unique given message for those who are beside us, behind us, and in front of us, for we can always touch someone's life regardless of where they are in their journey and where we are with ours.

I believe that as we are given experiences in our lives, as hard and cruel as they may be sometimes, they are there as events to shape us into the human beings we become, and if we allow ourselves to heal and look back at those experiences, the learning and gained insights we now have can be the lifeboat for others to hang on as they go through their own life experiences. In short, all the pain and suffering each one of us has experienced does not have to end in only that; we can use that pain and suffering to guide, educate, support, and heal others who are desperately wanting someone to understand and to become ambassadors for them and to them. Our pain can truly be our gift to humanity.

This is why I believe now with all my heart and soul that my psychotic episode in 1992 as a young adult and my recovery after ten sessions of electroconvulsive therapy and a diagnosis of bipolar disorder was an event and an experience I was given so that one day I could stand on my two feet holding hands with others who had been on the same journey and not feel alone. And I could extend my arms and heart to all those who were longing to be loved and understood. Who would have thought that the most painful and devastating experience my family and I would go through would one day become the experience I am most grateful for, the one that would become my legacy and gift to humanity?

I am sure you would agree with me that as a society, we have made great progress in many areas and have also removed the stigma we have toward many social issues like same-sex marriage, alcohol abuse, multi-racial marriages, and yet when it comes to mental illness, I believe you all would agree that we have lived in the darkness long enough.

So why is this so important and why now? Because the numbers are staggering and something must change. According to the National Institute of Mental Health, depression is the leading cause of disability worldwide and is a major contributor to the global burden on disease. In 2020 in the US alone, 52.9 million people (approximately one in five people) were affected by a mental illness, according to the NAMI (National Alliance of Mental Illness).[1] Most of them were affected by anxiety, major depression, and mood disorders, which have dramatic consequences not only for those affected but also for their families and their social- and work-related environments. According to the American Journal of Psychiatry, mental illness cost America an

---

1—NAMI: National Alliance on Mental Illness (homepage), accessed September 19, 2022, www.nami.org.

estimated $210 billion dollars in lost earnings per year.[2] Imagine how the economy would benefit from $210 billion dollars. As you can see, the impact to our communities and economy is greater than we think.

Mental disorders are by no means limited to a small group of predisposed individuals but are a major public health problem. In fact, mental illnesses are extremely common, and most importantly, the majority of them are treatable. For all these reasons, it is imperative that we reconsider the cost of mental disorders, the cost benefits of treatment and preventive interventions, and the benefit to ending the stigma on an illness that those who have it did not chose it.

Why has this become so important to me?

Because on a cold winter night in February of 1992, I suffered from a devasting full-blown psychotic episode where many inexplicable things happened including, jumping out of one-and-a-half-story window fully naked, and walking on the streets of the small town for who knows how long. It ended with me strapped to a security vest in a fully padded room at a psychiatry hospital with an incorrect diagnosis of schizophrenia and fully medicated to make me calm down.

My dad had to travel to Iowa to get me back to Mexico City where it would take six more months of hospitalization with twenty-four seven care by family members, many medication combinations, and the assistance of the board of psychiatry in Mexico City reviewing my case to finally come to the correct diagnosis of bipolar disorder. I would require ten sessions of electroconvulsive therapy to bring me back from the darkness and for me to be able to write this today.

How had this happened? I had been a healthy child from the day I was born. I was capable of making friends extremely easy

The truth is that six months prior to me going back to Iowa,

2—Thomas R. Insel, "Assessing the Economic Costs of Serious Mental Illness," The American Journal of Psychiatry, June 1, 2008, https://doi.org/10.1176/appi.ajp.2008.08030366.

all the indications of a deep, deep depression were present, and eventually it would cause me to spiral out of control on that cold winter night in 1992. My doctor also found out that mental illness was heavily present in our family's genetics, so all this made sense. This was a huge revelation. The family history and the behaviors I exhibited before I left were all indicators that something was not right, and if my parents would have known what to look for, things could have been different.[3]

This is why I am passionate about this cause. Armed with this experience and knowledge, my family and I have been able to intervene in many situations and provide comfort, hope, and enough information for those struggling to seek the help they need.

My life has been full of great experiences, and while not always happy experiences, I have to say I believe I have had a pretty good and happy life and have not been hospitalized since that original episode. I am the mother to two fantastic human beings, have been married to a wonderful man for over twenty-seven years, have been a successful business owner for the last sixteen years, and have become an author, trainer, and speaker—all despite my mental illness diagnosis . . . or as I like to see it, it has been all thanks to my diagnosis.

So if you are wondering why I would consider this a gift to my life and now a gift to others, it is very simple: I believe we are meant to do good with the experiences we are given, as painful as they may be. This is why since 2015 I have been sharing my story of recovery and hope as part of the Stop Stigma Sacramento Speakers Bureau. We are a group of approximately fifty individuals from all different walks of life and with different diagnoses who speak on a regular basis in several venues in our community. From schools to colleges and from small businesses to the US Army Corps of Engineers, our message is the same: Mental illness is not always what you think, it can be treated, you are not alone,

---

3—Read Claudia's story on *Faces of Mental Illness* available on Amazon.

and there is hope for a bright future despite your diagnosis. I want to make sure as many families as possible understand the signs of mental illness so they can find treatment for their loved ones before it is too late.

My involvement with this organization and my desire to stop the stigma on mental illness and the need to change the narrative around it led me to the creation of a global movement called Faces of Mental Illness[4] where many individuals from around the world come together to share their own personal stories, shining a different light on mental illness and therefore creating a brighter tomorrow for us all. It is through these stories that others have found peace in knowing they are not alone and where many others (including family members) have found out what may be happening to them or their loved ones so that they can seek the professional help they need.

My legacy is not of money, properties, or status, and yet I believe it is as important if not more than all those things combined. Fighting to stop the stigma on mental illness and impact the views of those who do not understand it and change the lives of those who live with it has truly become my mission and my legacy. My legacy is to provide information, give hope, and create the space where people like me feel safe, loved, understood, and supported.

Mental illness chose me for a reason, and now I know exactly why. My mental illness changed my life, and because of that, I can now change the lives of others so we can all enjoy a brighter tomorrow! Never in a million years would I have guessed that the most devastating experience in my life would become my most cherished gift, for it carried with it the seed to create change. If this is not an amazing gift; I really do not know what is.

4—*Faces of Mental Illness* available on Amazon.

ABOUT CLAUDIA FERNANDEZ-NIEDZIELSKI

From an early age, Claudia became obsessed with positive information and positive quotes after her father introduced her and her brothers to books that would inspire them to always strive to be the best they could be.

Claudia is a survivor and a woman who has learned to thrive despite the many challenges she has faced. She loves her parents, brothers, children, husband, and extended family with all her heart and continues to learn how to live a life full of passion and in full harmony with herself. Claudia is currently on a quest to be the best version of herself and fully master that. She has a genuine and profound impact on others as she mentors and leads them to live life to the fullest and shares the tools she has utilized on her own personal search for meaning, self-discovery, understanding, and compassion for herself and others and her deep self-worth.

She is a Jack Canfield Success Principles certified trainer and a Barret Value Center certified practitioner and consultant. She is an entrepreneur, an accomplished speaker, and #1 international best-selling author.

To learn more about Claudia Fernandez-Niedzielski, you can visit her website at:

www.ClaudiaImpactsLives.com

To book Claudia as a speaker or work with her, please contact her directly at:

ClaudiaImpactsLives@gmail.com
(916) 248-3004

FALL IN LOVE WITH LIFE

Angela Germano

Heart in throat
Palms pulsing
Eye twitching
Taste your dry mouth
See nothing
"Do it. Do it," the voice whispers.

Tongue the upper lip
Take a moment
Bite the lower lip softly
That was unexpected
Focus
Now, let's go

Let us fall in love

But people are tricky
Lots of moving parts
Unexplainable mind shifts
Ever-changing hearts

I want to fall in love

I want to love
I want a love

Comfortable, secure, confident love
Feel-the-smile-from-the-inside kinda love
Laughter, that calms
A few breaths, and the world is more at peace
Reliable, always-there, reassuring love

Wait—what's that I see
Let me readjust my lens
Oh, the perspective shift—
Drumroll please . . .

Say it, I am in love.

Yes, there it is
Fall in love with Life.

**"Who is this lady encouraging me to fall in love
with my crazy life? She doesn't know my life."**

True. So let me tell you about mine. Not about the "palm trees, bay waves, and breeze with the song of the seagulls waking me up in my beach house" dream come true. Not about how I became a #1 international best-selling author, multiple times. Not about how I am a professional writer, award-winning educator, doctorate student, mom, friend, good neighbor, and fun spirit. Not about how I am breathing it all in as I enjoy the sweet, salty air and am so appreciative that the rhythm of my life has brought me to these moments. Nope. Let's talk about the raw, bare-naked, tumultuous truth of how I fell in love with life.

I was born into heroic beginnings; it didn't look good, but I feel like if there was an audience watching my life, they'd be rooting for me. So, grab your popcorn.

"My life sucks! I could never fall in love with it."

I look back on pictures, and I was a happy little girl; I took becoming a big sister seriously. I was a dancer—ballet, tap, acrobatics, jazz, pointe. I was an eager-to-learn, conscientious student who loved art. But of course, the polaroids don't show the government cheese, the abusive household, and the cancer that took over our lives. No one wanted to see that reality, but my young eyes did.

I saw my dad's sorrow, saw him picket. Watched him psych himself up and fill out job applications with hope. I admired his tenacity reading endless plumbing books, furnace repair manuals, studying auto mechanic magazines all to fix the prized possessions we still had. I remember handing him a makeshift plastic bag of a raincoat as he rode a bike off to work odd jobs the next town over. He didn't make excuses, always worked hard, and kept going, taking nothing for granted, *or at least it seemed*.

When I was in fourth grade, my mom was diagnosed with cancer. She had fallen at a party and complained about her back hurting. No one would have thought that this undiagnosed breast cancer had traveled to her back and around her spine, but it did. That's how it was explained to me. My mom was always perfectly composed, but I could see my dad's fear and physically felt his relentless frustration for the next five years.

With all my mom was battling, she took on my dad's frustration as well. Life can be completely unfair, cruel, and uncontrollable. My mom's cancer came back with a vengeance, twice more. As my dad was in and out of our house, I scheduled doctor appointments and transportation, attended chemotherapy treatments, gave my mom her needles (she had two IVs daily since her veins were shot over the years), tended to my five-year-younger sister and her education, as well as took care of our household. No friends were allowed over. Who would want to see the horror behind this straight-A smiling dancer as I hustled through elementary and middle school?

She held on as long as she could, I know this. She always

prayed for life a little bit longer: "I just want to make it long enough to see you walk through that archway in your cap and gown, Angela." My mom suffered a stroke or two during this, and finally after five years in our dreadful home, she passed away on the very night I pushed her away and went out with my friends instead. I was beginning my ninth-grade year.

There was a lot of blame within our so-called family. Fighting over money, ugly accusations, and truths surfacing. My father decided to leave it all behind and start fresh, the best he could for his own self-preservation. He took my five-year-younger sister with him and moved five hours away. Neither set of grandparents, no aunts or uncles really *wanted* me to live with them. After some time, my next-door neighbor took me in and cared for me my senior year of high school.

I was tormented growing up. Heck, I was pushed into turmoil and then held under water, barely able to catch a breath. But being given an opportunity to join another household was pretty awesome. I witnessed how some took that home and those parents for granted, and I vowed never to do that, to anyone or any home. To this day, I hold true to that and I have no tolerance for anyone taking any person, place, or thing for granted.

"That was my childhood. I can choose my adulthood."

My past was just that, my past. Although I was rooted in that turmoil, I learned that I could control myself. I vowed to nurture and love myself beyond words can fathom. I learned to be wholeheartedly independent. I learned to see the value in everything—every moment of life, of every experience, of every opportunity. I fell in love with life—trusting the unraveling, twisting, relentless ride.

My being had been challenged immensely at a very young age for years, and my soul will continue to be put through the wringer, but I can control my perception, my understanding. I give it the value: I can control my energy and how I choose to utilize it. After all, I had been granted the gift of life, and I was on a mission to live it up for my mom.

"What if I can't do it alone?"

That is the beauty of life: we are so fortunate to be surrounded by souls. At their core, we all want to belong, to be comforted, accepted. Look around at what life offers.

Along my journey, I allowed teachers and coaches to comfort me as well. I fondly remember so many of them. My math teachers taught me it was applaudable to respectfully challenge someone intellectually. I would sit in the front of the class and ask genuine questions because I wanted to readily apply the lessons. Although they seemed to get frustrated with all my questioning, I knew it was because they needed to think on their feet all while the little voice inside their head was probably saying, *How in the world is she going to use the Pythagorean theory or calculus?* I earned the Math Award Senior Night. Truth be told, I thought they disliked me, but they assured me, "No way, you challenged me to be my best version of a teacher, every day in class." I was a gift to them. So even though in my younger homelife questioning authority was seen as a negative, it actually was a high-level skill that my instructors appreciated. They were such an absolute gift to me.

And so I saw life's challenges as positive opportunities, gifts to be unwrapped and cherished. This was a pivotal moment as I started to fall in love with life, the intelligent, reassuring trickster.

My coaches ensured I took on every life opportunity as well. They encouraged me to run for leadership roles within not just my school but outside as well. This allowed me entry into scholarship competitions to help me pay for college. My coaches made sure that we competed on dozens of college campuses so I could get multiple tastes of a new life that could be mine and made sure I knew that I deserved it. They pushed me to audition for acting and debate scholarships. I actually credit my debate coach for helping me discover my alma mater, Monmouth University.

He actually set up a tournament there so I could explore the campus, and it felt like . . . my future. The feeling was mutual because I was accepted and awarded multiple scholarships, as well as campus employment. That assistance paired with the grants I earned from my high school community allowed my dream of college to come true—a new life that I knew I deserved. I kept telling myself to believe in myself, that I could and would excel in this new life. And I owe that voice, my voice, all to my teachers. I made the choice to acknowledge and listen to life guiding, encouraging, and providing for me.

I remember going through a bad breakup with my boyfriend of six years and knocking on my soccer coach's door, past midnight, two years after I had graduated. The nonjudgmental comfort she supplied changed my life. It showed me that what you feel in your heart, you can show that. The love that you feel, you can show that off.

I had gone through the stages of fear, blame, feelings of inadequacies, worthlessness, and awkwardness, but life picked me up relentlessly. Life kept on showing up, and with the support of trusted adults, I started cautiously dating, learning to trust, relaxing, believing in myself, and learning that the world works in mysterious ways, so I better listen carefully. I was ready to show off my love for life.

I not only went to college, but I took advantage of every opportunity in each nook and cranny life gave me. The love that I was open to receiving in all these different ways filled my cup, and I then could fill others'. I embraced the love. I saw how life's challenges could be so easily perceived as a negative, and I wanted to use my love to shield others from sorrow and pain. My love became my super strength; it was limitless with no kryptonite. See how I was falling hard for life?

Now that I had my dream-come-true college opportunity, I safeguarded it every bit of the way. I was in total control, protecting my new life. I went to bed early, submitted my assignments promptly, stayed on the straight and narrow, and was looking to study abroad and land internships as a first-year student.

I remember getting a phone call from my dad.

As I was finally in my own space, under my own rules, he needed me. Just as my teachers had indirectly taught me, I took on the challenge respectfully and took the call. Being there for my dad made me an even stronger person. Life gave me that gift of an opportunity.

That summer, I lived with my dad and my sister. As my sister was clumsily navigating through her high school years, they both needed me, and it felt good to bond with my dad. In an odd way, I became his teacher, guiding him to a healthier life, which I took great pride in. I shared my goal to start working within the communication field. As luck would have it, there was a radio station walking distance from his house, and he encouraged me to introduce myself. I took his tip, and it worked out. I became a radio DJ, news reporter, and even got paid for some of my news reports from The Associated Press. This was *huge* for me. (Still to this day, my dad is rooting me on, sharing his wisdom.) Another dream was coming true, all because I made the choice to take that call from my dad, because I made the choice to open my heart, because I had learned from my teachers to seek out each opportunity to make my dreams come true. I was falling hard for life.

I didn't stop. I continued to stay focused on my newfound love affair with life. I went on to study theatre at Thames Valley University in London and worked as a hair model and Pizza Hut taste tester to have a richer experience abroad. Upon returning to Monmouth, in only my second year, I joined the Forensics and Debate team and continued to travel and experience more than just my college campus. Once again, my teachers and coaches believed in me and pushed me to excel. They'd often dig for deeper meaning in my responses, causing me to do the same, to make sure I was staying true to myself and following my intellectual curiosity. I was rooted in myself, living for me and believing in me, even when my beliefs and desires were different. I am still in touch with many of these beautiful souls, and they are still guiding and looking out for me. I trusted life wholeheartedly.

I went on to be part of The Washington Center, one of the most reputable and sought-after academic seminars and paid internship experiences in communications. Once I was accepted into this program, companies actually competed to employ me and I got to choose. It was an amazing experience—being wanted. My own family didn't want me after my mom died, but these strangers saw my merit and potential and wanted me.

I attended numerous congressional events and became a valuable member of the environmental and educational team at a DC Public Relations agency while taking a full college course load studying congressional law at George Mason University and not only graduating magna cum laude but being offered a job at the same firm in Irvine, California. This brilliant group of professionals believed in me, but they weren't the only ones. Monmouth University offered me a hefty scholarship to continue my studies and earn my master's in public and corporate communications. Education, with all its open-hearted mentors along the way, had afforded me a new life, a better life, one I had control over. And I could not pass up an opportunity for more. But once again there was a choice, and it was mine to make with all my open mind and loving heart.

Falling in love with life, like trusting it wholeheartedly and seeing it for all of its boundless opportunities is nothing short of amazing. Making it through a "decrepit" town with a bad reputation and even worse reality of family abuse, losing my mom to a five-year battle with cancer, and being rejected by family, homeless as a high school student, I managed to exceed expectations, win numerous awards across careers, and am still rising.

At my first book signing, I was asked to be a public relations consultant for an international expeditionary healthcare company and successfully was part of a team launching them into the #1 spot, recognized and revered as the experts they are amid the 2020 coronavirus pandemic. Even though I am not a doctor, I was able to help people by bringing medical attention to them during this horrific time in history. I felt like I was doing my part to help the world. Letting that sink in, I definitely felt the magic of being in love with life.

One dream after the next came true: owning my dream beach house in a gorgeous community, having a rewarding educational career, being interviewed multiple times for my positivity, earning a doctoral scholarship to get my PhD, becoming an associate producer for a documentary series that encompasses all that I believe in and aspire for others. Now I'm on stage at movie premieres, attending film festivals, writing TV pilots and movie scripts. I am loving life, and I know you can too.

I could have fallen prey to negativity, unwarranted fear, and self-doubt, but I chose to fall in love with all the opportunities, moments, and gifts of life.

**"Lean in with calm, confidence, and grace.
You got this."**

Growing up was not easy, and it may not be for anyone. We all have fears. I feared marriage, having children, and now I have the most amazing loves in my life that make each moment more incredible than the next. We all have our own unique set of challenges, from disadvantaged neighborhoods, loss, stereotypes, untrustworthy friends, being abandoned, feeling isolated or unwanted, the list goes on and on. Much of that you can't control—and that is fine.

But what does the inner voice say to you? That's your voice. That's the writer of your story. You have all the choice, all the power. You have the power to choose a positive mindset and shift full throttle toward loving life. Keep your eyes open, your heart open, your mind open to all the guiding light offering illumination and allowing you to rise above.

Being in love with life feels so good; it is the best relationship. People ask where I get my nonstop energy from, and sincerely, I am giddy getting to live another day of life. I will not take it for granted. I am a positive force to be reckoned with. I attract many with my friendly, ambitious nature, living life to its fullest, and I can show up bright and strong for my loved ones. I can give so much more, truly in love with life.

When you are in love with life, you are present in the moment—these gracious gifts of time. You embrace all the feels and questions, to reflect and grow. You recognize that these are the seeds to nourish your life. Sometimes you will see the blossom and sometimes your love will transpire to others, bringing them support, comfort, and nourishment. Celebrate it all, live life to its fullest, even and perhaps most importantly through the challenges.

Fall in love with life
"Do it. Do it," the voice whispers.
Tongue the upper lip
Take a moment
Bite the lower lip softly
Muster up the courage

Power is in your choices
Don't let fear contain you
It's your outlook,
your wants, your desires
You have all you need,
All you want and it's plentiful
It is reliable

Promise

Fall in love with life,
Appreciate and respect it and it will catch you
It will comfort you; it will cheer you on

It will raise you up

Keep going with all your heart
Go through it, just get through it
Be there for yourself
Shine your brightest,
Love with all you are!
Fall in love with life.

This is my legacy, and I present it to you: my gift.

ABOUT ANGELA GERMANO

Associate producer of *Authentic Conversations: Deep Talk with the Masters*, #1 international best-selling and award-winning author in the Inspired Impact Book Series including *Women Who Rise, Women Who Illuminate,* and *Leading with Legacy.*

Angela Germano was featured in The Jersey Storytellers Project, part of the *USA Today Network,* and is often a guest on educational and mental health podcasts.

An award-winning teacher by day, college professor and multi-faceted professional writer by night, she raises her two children the best she can with her supportive husband. Graduating magna cum laude with a master's in public and corporate communications from Monmouth University, she's been an award-winning debater, marketer, actress, constitutional law student, drive-time radio personality, and always a coach devoted to positively impacting people's lives so they can achieve their dreams.

Angela has served on the Monmouth University board of directors and is involved with multiple charities such as Ronald McDonald House, American Cancer Society, and UNICEF. She is noted as having a true teaching talent: putting students at ease, increasing their confidence, and allowing them to learn for the long-term. She focuses on embracing teaching as an opportunity to inspire leadership, giving voice and choice to students through knowledge, exemplars, and opportunity.

Angela is also an inspirational speaker highlighting the specific topics of overcoming adversity, building confidence, and leadership as well as an organizer and grant writer for Selfie Celebrations where children practice positive self-worth activities such as yoga, meditation, positive affirmations, goal-setting, and vision boards.

To learn more, you can reach Angela Germano at:

angelagermanopositivity@gmail.

AN EMERGING LEGACY

Jeanie Griffin

"No legacy is so rich as honesty."

—William Shakespeare

U nraveling the story of people, history, and past civilizations fascinated me even in middle school. I was mesmerized by the advancements of entire cultures only to wonder why and how they had vanished. The mystery of who they were, what they stood for, and the legacies they left captured my imagination.

In high school I collected song lyrics and poems and rewrote them in a journal. These lyrics and poems were my "voice" back then. They put into words feelings and thoughts that I could not articulate in those days. A poem that haunted me was Carl Sandburg's *Four Preludes on Playthings in the Wind*. Mr. Sandburg tells of a boastful nation who paid women to chant "We are the greatest city, the greatest nation, nothing like us ever was." His depiction of this once great nation where only the dust and rats remain caused me to wonder if America could or would vanish like the others. And why would it happen? What would be our legacy? What would be my personal legacy?

I love to study history because it is the study of people, and

I love to study people's behavior. No wonder I became a high school history teacher for a time and now a psychotherapist.

Growing up, when I heard the term *legacy,* I thought of what civilizations left behind. I marveled when exploring old ruins and historical places. It may be strange to some but I like to learn about people who came before me by visiting old graveyards. Previously, the term "legacy" included a person's name immortalized for making a large financial contribution or building a hospital or museum or something grand like that. It never occurred to me that leaving a legacy might mean leaving something *in* people rather than *for* people.

To me, leaving a legacy and being a leader did not necessarily equate. People had always told me I was a leader. They were sure of it because they had drawn inspiration from the challenges I had overcome, but I couldn't see it. Some said I was a leader because I was strong and an independent thinker. Others told me I was a leader because my astrological sign was a cardinal sign. Still others said I was a leader because I was bossy. Perhaps all are true for me. Dolly Parton, in the 1997 book, *The Most Important Thing I Know*, stated, "If your actions create a legacy that inspires others to dream more, learn more, do more and become more, then, you are an excellent leader."

I did not plan to be a leader or to leave a legacy. I was merely trying to get through what showed up for me each day. It never occurred to me that I was growing into leadership or leaving a legacy *in* people when they observed my thoughts, actions, values, or teachings. Today I can honestly say I have and do inspire people to dream more, do more, and become more, but I never set out to do so. How do I do that? Why do I do that?

I am a storyteller. You can read a brief story of my life in a collaborative book in the *Inspired Impact Book Series, Women Who Rise* found on my website and Amazon. I have been through a lot, and finally one day I admitted I was unhappy, discontent, angry, and tired of running my life on sheer willpower. Discontent is not a bad thing, I have discovered. It stirred me to examine my life. Of course, initially I looked outside myself and blamed everyone and everything else for my unhappiness. But then one of my spiritual mentors helped me see I was the common denominator in every unhappy situation. She encouraged me to look inside and take inventory of my part in those situations. While such examination was a daunting task, I began to see where I was at fault.

I tried to control everything and everyone in my life because it supported the illusion that I could make myself safe if only I could manage my life well. I experienced a lot of heartache as a child, so I swore I would never let anyone or anything hurt me again. I was raised in an alcoholic home, and at the time of my birth, my family was homeless, though we did not call it that in those days. I was the last of four children, and while I knew I was loved, I always had the sense of being one more burden for my parents.

I made two decisions before I was six, which would later put me in a position to be hurt. First decision: I told myself it was my job to make my parents happy so my dad would not drink and my mother would not be depressed. The second decision I made was to switch to magical thinking or fantasy when circumstances became hard or hurtful. Both of these decisions showed up in my thoughts as two rules or old ideas: 1) If X, then Y, and 2) When X, then I'm gonna Y. E.g., If I can be cute enough, smart enough, sweet enough, then my dad won't drink. Or when I grow up, then I'm gonna never marry an alcoholic. I lived by those old ideas well into my late thirties trying to force solutions that fit. I was going to "make this work."

My willpower made me a successful high school history/government teacher and even earned me Teacher of the Year. Students who were not in my classes asked to come in and listen. I took up causes of injustice and championed them. I could leap tall buildings in a single bound and keep Saturn on its axis. If I kept busy, then I would not feel.

My willpower and tenacity left me lonely, unhappy, and discontent. I rode the coattails of my mother's faith when at thirteen, my father left and at fifteen, he died. I totally turned my back on God when at twenty-one, my mother died and a friend's six-year-old was stolen out of the basement of her church, raped, murdered, and tossed into a dumpster. I was unwilling to listen to anyone. I had decided I would not need a God, and I trusted no one. I had few close friends with whom I was honest.

After twenty years, I divorced, but I was a determined I would give my daughter everything I had not had emotionally and materially as a child.

What on earth could I give to her? How could I avoid choices that would hurt her? How could I do a better job as a parent? At this time, I finally realized how alcoholism had shaped many of my thoughts, feelings, and actions. I was exhausted, so I finally surrendered to the fact that I was Fresh Outta Plans and nothing in my bag of tricks worked anymore.

With pent-up anger and rage, I finally went to a twelve-step program, not because I wanted to but because my sisters suggested it. A few women looked past my resentments, fear, and hurt and loved me when I could not love myself. I was not happy about the idea of me respecting a higher power or concept of God as I understood but I was willing to listen to suggestions because I had what I now know as the gift of desperation. I desperately wanted my daughter's life to be better.

It was suggested I be honest, open-minded, and willing, so eventually I was. I threw myself into *living* the twelve-step spiritual program. I went into therapy. I went back to school for a master's degree and became an addictions psychotherapist. For over thirty years, I have worked with people with addictions and with their families. I share honestly about my own story. I teach compassion toward the loved ones with addictions as well as boundary setting. I challenge the families to be willing to change, as they ask the addicted one to, and I offer hope to all. I have taught workshops to thousands of families. With willingness, a faith, an honest community, and by following directions, anyone and any family can put addiction in remission and live a life filled with peace, joy, and love no matter what chaos and drama is happening around them. I am living proof of it, and I help others get there too.

At the age of fifty, I ran away from home and moved to Los Angeles. One day while driving down Venice Blvd, I heard an advertisement on the radio inviting people to a gathering of the shaman and healers from all over the world in Big Bear, CA. I had no idea where Big Bear was or what the gathering was about, but my intuition said, "You have to go!" The next moment, I was investigating the event on Google. I found the name of a woman associated with the event, Valerie, who lived in Topanga. I called her and asked for an appointment. We set a time and then she asked, "May I dream for you?" I had no clue what that meant, but I thought, *Sure, knock yourself out—whatever that means.* I said, "Of course."

On the drive up to her house, I gave myself permission to leave immediately if she turned out to be a wacko or wanted me to eat a raw chicken or something else weird. We greeted each other pleasantly as I entered. "I am not sure why I am here, but I think we have work together," I said. She looked me straight in the eyes and stated, "You have come to us to teach you how to be an elder." I burst into tears. I knew she was right but had no idea what it meant. We worked for a few months after that visit I began a three-year training in shamanism with her. I use shamanic practices today. During my studies, I met another wonderful mentor, Deena, who startled me upon meeting her. She, too, looked me directly in the eyes and said, "Prepare to be 60". I asked, "What?". She repeated it, "Prepare to be 60". I laughed and made a joke that she did not find the least bit funny. Her stare held as she continued, "By then you will have gathered a people who need an elder." I began to cry. I knew she was right but had no clue how that would unfold.

Working with those women and others in the shamanic tradition of nature deepened my growing reaffirmation of faith. Connecting to all beings and learning how to use helping spirits solidified my faith in both the visible and invisible assisting us on this life journey. Today I know The Oneness is always present and available to help us.

Today I show people and inspire others to dream more, to take action, and to do more to use their talents and gifts to make a positive difference in the world. My business is called FRESH OUTTA PLANS®, and my website is https://freshouttaplans.com. I have developed a three-pillar method I use in my own life every day. From my experience, I teach others. The FRESH OUTTA PLANS Three Pillar Program of Untangle the Mind, Experience the Invisible, and Connect with Community teaches people to feel peace even in the middle of chaos. My podcast, *The Recovered Therapist* can be found wherever you listen to podcasts. It is not a traditional podcast because I do not interview anyone. I pick a topic and talk about it for four to twenty minutes in an effort to invite people to think about the topic. Check it out. You can also listen to over 75 videos called #SeniorJail on my YouTube channel, Jeanie Griffin. The name comes from being locked down "in jail" during the pandemic.

I am reminded daily the spiritual life is not a theory. You have to take action. Some spiritual action tools I use daily and teach others to use are: Go outside and watch an ant or a squirrel. They trust and live in the present. Practice listening and acting on your intuition. Leave things better because you have been there. Practice compassion. Be *a part of*, instead of being *apart from*. Connect with community so you can be supported as well as be of service. Admit your mistakes and make changes. Take responsibility. Align your individual will with your Higher Self or a Higher Power of your understanding. Share hope. Share your gifts. If you follow these tools in whatever order, you will begin to experience peace even in the middle of chaos. Your life's purpose will unfold. Before you know it, you will be a leader leaving your legacy *in* people. You, too, will have gathered a people who need an elder. Join me as we make the world a better place. I wish you peace and blessings.

ABOUT JEANIE GRIFFIN

Jeanie Griffin is a #1 international best-selling author, keynote speaker, VIP retreat leader, shamanic practitioner, mental health counselor, and addictions trauma psychotherapist. She is the founder and CEO of the Los Angeles business FRESH OUTTA PLANS®. She holds a master's degree and is professionally licensed in California and Texas. People come to her with spiritual questions, challenging relationships, codependency, substance abuse challenges, anxiety, and depression. She has the right combination of compassion, humor, and honesty.

Jeanie Griffin has appeared on *Divorce Talk* with Dr. Sue, *Where All Things Are Possible* with Kate Butler, *Everybody* with Dr. Angela Sadler Williamson, *The Relaxed Dog* with Robert Ober and *We're All Psychic* with Lisa Rusczyk.

She is an assistant producer *Authentic Conversations: Deep Talk with the Masters*, a documentary written, directed, and produced by Dr. Angela Sadler Williamson featuring Jack Canfield, Patty Aubery, and Kate Butler. It is the first in a series of documentaries about the importance of having authentic conversations.

Website: freshouttaplans.com
Facebook Group: FRESH OUTTA PLANS Community Group
TikTok: @freshouttaplans
Instagram: @jeaniegriffinla
Podcast: The Recovered Therapist with Jeanie Griffin
Amazon Books: *Women Who Rise* by Jeanie Griffin

IF I ONLY HAD SOME COURAGE:
THE LION IN OUR MIDST

Laurel Joakimides

The Desert
05:00 August 2019

Quietly I twist the doorknob leading into the garage, excited about catching my flight from Phoenix to Lake Tahoe to attend USAPA's Pickleball Bootcamp when the landline rings, breaking the quiet stillness of the early-morning hour. *Who in the world . . .?* I quickly make my way to answer and find it's Joy, my youngest daughter. My heart suddenly pounds so hard and fast, it's screaming, "Red Alert!" and I can hardly breathe as I put the receiver to my ear. Two days earlier, Joy had said her good-byes to her youngest daughter, Chloe, after helping Chloe move into her college dorm room at University of Colorado at Boulder.

"MOM!" Joy screamed. She is sobbing hysterically, and I have trouble understanding her. "Mom, are you there? I've . . . trying to reach you!" Her sobs are so terrifying, and I can't understand what she is saying.

"Honey, I'm here, I'm right here. I'm having trouble

hearing . . . Yes, I can hear you now. I'm right here. Is it Chloe? Honey, is Chloe . . . Joy, please let me know, is Chloe okay?" My own voice is beginning to break. *Please, God . . .*

"Mom, [*inaudible*] is dead and [*inaudible*] . . ."

"Honey, what? I can't—please try—"

"Momma, [*inaudible*] and [*inaudible*] is dead . . . [sobbing] and . . . Mom? Momma, are you there? Mom [sobbing] . . . can you hear me?!"

One hour later, I am sitting on the first flight out of Tucson heading in a different direction.

When Kate Butler approached me and asked if I would consider co-authoring a chapter for an upcoming book, she said that she envisions me drafting a story around my resiliency in overcoming life's challenges. The Road to Hope, she suggested. My negative thought pattern kicked in, took off running at lightning speed, and had a field day.

"HOPE?!" Hope? *Yes, I bounce back quickly, but every four stinking months something shows up and it cripples me! For crying out loud, I'm trying to get out of this desert, and at every turn something blows up!*

I pull myself together and put my recording on pause. Inhale. Exhale. I listened long and hard to all that Kate was offering. I did not want to pass up this opportunity, but at the same time I was the right fit for the topic—especially now. I said yes before we ended the conversation.

Only a handful of people in my life know about what happened that fateful day in 2019, Kate being one of them when I shared some of the details of my story with her in August 2020. Today, while still in the middle of writing this piece, I am convinced that without Kate crossing my path at exactly the right time, I would not be here with you, living out my life purpose. I believe with my whole heart that God (call it Source, higher power, Spirit, the universe, whatever you choose) moved all the pieces in the universe in order for me to do the work He has called me to do. Kate is the vehicle; you the reader are here by divine plan. On three separate occasions when I was threatening to throw in the towel, God said, "No. Not yet. I know the plans I have for you. Take out your journal and write." As you may have read in my previous story, "If I Only Had a Brain," in *Women Who Empower*, you'll remember that I'm sometimes slow on the uptake, or how stinking thinking keeps me from moving forward. I cannot help but think how much different my life would look today if I only had some courage.

* * *

From kindergarten and a fairy princess to wicked witches and falling in ditches, there's a hole in my heart and my brain is in tatters; oh, for the courage to pick up the pieces that matter; if I had me a pair of some red ruby slippers, I could travel this road and meet that smart Wizard. Walk with me, walk with me, stay with me please. I'm alone on this journey, I'm scared, and it matters.

—Laurel Joakimides (2020)

The sheer magnitude of the grief filling my heart and soul the days and months following that fateful day is beyond one's grasp. There wasn't a playbook available with instructions on how to proceed. My prayers seemed to be falling on deaf ears. There were nights, many of them, when I would stumble out of bed at one, two, or three in the morning, wailing with grief, begging God for release. The tasks before me were so overwhelming and much more than I could ever possibly imagine doing that it was all I *could* do to put on a stoic face by day, only to fall on my knees in the early hours of morning and cry out desperately for some help. On some days I would find myself standing at the ocean's door feeling so lost and empty inside, I would outwardly scream, "God, WHERE ARE YOU?! You promise you will never leave us nor forsake us! WHERE ARE YOU?! ARE YOU LISTENING?!"

One early-morning hour in late October, I sat down on the floor leaning my back against the side of the bed, and with tear-filled eyes and an aching heart, I conducted a one-way conversation with God. "Please, Lord, I'm asking you for some help and some guidance today. This is what I need . . ." and I laid it all out before Him. I shared all my frustrations and all my concerns, including the time constraints I was under. I spelled out in detail all the things I had to do that were scaring me. I also added that I just wanted to go home. "Lord, I ask all this in Jesus' name. Holy Spirit, come. Amen"

I sat there on the floor for a long time after with my eyes closed, listening to the sounds of the house settling. In my silent stillness came the following: "Ask Amelia for the Bible you gave her four years ago. Read it to Jacob."

"Okay," I whispered aloud and climbed back into bed. *Maybe I'll turn reading a story from the Bible into a nightly ritual. Why not? Maybe it will help him calm down before putting him into bed. I'll call it our special story time. Yes, that sounds good. For five minutes each night the first week and then ten minutes the second week, I'll read to him and see where it leads.*

Note: Jacob (not his real name) is my adult special needs non-verbal grandson. Since infancy, bedtime has always been a challenge for him. He also has difficulty adapting to changes in his daily routine. Understandably, the first week of our new nightly routine of story time was rocky. By the second week, it dawned on him that I wasn't going away, and little by little his behavior began to change. He was calmer and curious about the book in my hands. I kept reading for ten minutes, no matter what. Upon closing the Bible, I guided him to his bedside, helped him into bed, said our prayers, and before exiting his room I would run my hand down the side of his body from head to toe to let him know I was leaving, and then turn off the light. By the end of the third week, Jacob helped himself into bed, said "amen" after our prayers and he said, "Night" to me as I was leaving the room.

"Good night, Jacob. I love you," I responded and turned off the light. Just before closing his door, he said, "You." *Thank you, Lord. We're reaching him.*

In early November, something shifted. Doors began opening, phone calls were being returned, calls were coming in on my phone while driving in the car, offering some sort of aid or assistance, and small miracles (angels) were showing up all around me—around us. Jacob was coming up with new words. There were moments of laughter again, and sometimes outright silliness. One evening Jacob walked up to me while I was having dinner and put his arm around my shoulder. Pulling me in a little closer, he said, "Story." When I told him it wasn't night-nighttime yet and we would have story time when we go upstairs for bed, he removed his arm from around my shoulder and said, "Tired," and made sounds as if he were snoring. "You're not tired, you joker!" I said to him. He laughed at his own antics with his way of laughter, a loud *hah, hah, hah!*

He's communicating on a much different level now! Thank you!

My heart was filling up with joy, hope, and gratitude that everything was working out as it was supposed to despite all the difficult circumstances I could see around me daily. The dense fog had lifted, and I no longer felt scared about all that still lay ahead.

It would be four months before my dog, Morgan, and I pulled into the driveway of our home in Tucson at dusk on December 23, 2019. My work was only partially complete; however, before making the return trip, I needed to pack some warmer clothes and other personal effects, plus I wanted my own car with me. What I really wanted in this moment was to disappear in my own house for a few days to have some desperately needed downtime.

I quickly unpacked the rental car and left it outside in the driveway. Jerry, my husband, driving home separately in his own car, estimated his arrival time to be somewhere around two or three the following morning. I welcomed the time alone in the house.

I hesitated to open a text message that just beeped through on my cell phone. It was Cheryl, my neighbor, from across the street. We became quick friends as soon as she and her husband, Max, moved into their new home two weeks after Jerry and I moved into ours.

"I saw the car in the driveway and hesitated about disturbing you," she texted, "but I really need to see you. I'm just outside. May I come in?"

"Yes," I texted back. "The door is unlocked, just come in. Are you alone?"

Within seconds, Cheryl stepped inside, closed the door behind her, walked over to where I was standing in the kitchen, and wrapped her arms tightly around me. "It's just me," she said. "Max doesn't need to be here right now. I need to be here with you. We've been praying for you. We don't have to talk. I just need to hold you. I'm glad you made it home safely. It's all going to be okay."

It may have been as long as five minutes that Cheryl rocked me gently. Her embrace felt like oxygen to me, and I clung to her as though she were my life support system. All the pent-up fear, doubt, angst, emptiness inside bubbled to the surface as we stood there. I can still feel Cheryl's arms holding me together as I unleashed my broken soul.

The following morning, a small live plant was waiting for me on the front porch. The shrub was in the shape of a tiny Christmas tree, adorned with a couple of small ornaments and a card. "We didn't want you and Jerry to be without a Christmas tree. Let us know if you need anything. Blessings, from Max and Cheryl"

As I sat on the living room couch admiring and holding the beautiful little Christmas tree on my lap, I whispered the words from Isaiah 61:3 (NIV), "and there will be beauty from the ashes."

Lord, I don't know why you made me come here to the desert in the first place, and I don't understand why you're not letting me leave if that's what you're doing. But for now, thank you for getting me here safely and for everything and everyone you put on my path to help me along the way. I now know I can depend on you to lead me places I've never been before, to places where you want me to go. I'll try not to blow it. In my heart, I know that you will keep your promise and turn these ashes into something beautiful. I don't know when, or where, or why, or how you're going to do it, but I know you keep your Word. You always have and always will even if you don't do it in this lifetime. Please forgive me for my times of doubt. Amen.

It's been three years since that fateful day in August 2019, and three more attempts to leave this desert and all have failed. It's been enough to get me to pause and look back over the past seven or eight years. Oddly, a pattern of crisis happened in a four-month cycle. *What am I missing? This block must have something to do with why I'm unable to draft my story about the Road to Hope. What am I missing, Lord? What am I pretending not to know? What's it costing me? STOP! Wait a second. You're not alone on this journey; you've never been alone! Wake up. Open your eyes! He's been carrying you!*

Flashback: The Lion in Our Midst

Let me take you back to an important event in June 2014. A friend invited me to meet her for coffee at a new place that had just opened along the lake. She wanted to share her excitement of becoming a vision-driven transformational coach. "Wow, Joyce. How exciting for you," I said. She asked if I would be willing to be her guinea pig so she could complete the requirements to become a certified facilitator. "This style of leadership development is right up your alley," she said. "What do you think?"

One week later, we began working together through the five-week training schedule. I was excited to be learning from this former full-time professor at Azusa Pacific University in California. What I especially admired about Joyce, who was seventy-five years young at the time, is that she still had a burning desire to learn, grow, contribute, and serve.

A couple weeks into the process, I began to question the purpose for asking so many personal questions in the homework assignments. From my perspective, the questions seemed too invasive. Joyce assured me that all were necessary and encouraged me to keep going, which of course I did, but truthfully, only half-heartedly. After another week or so when we were about halfway through the process, Joyce handed me a thick packet filled with five or six homework assignments. She said everything was due the following week. The detailed instructions had me going back and forth between homework #1, and #2, and incorporating homework #3 and #4 to "magically" produce a life purpose statement! Seriously?! I spent hours on the homework! At the end, not only was I disappointed that I wasn't able to articulate what my purpose in life is, I didn't have a clue how to pull it out of the homework assignments. I couldn't "fake it till I make it" with this high-caliber professor!

When we met the following week, all I had written down was that my purpose in life is to be a teacher.

"That's your spiritual gift," she responded. "What's your purpose? You need to write out your life purpose in a declarative statement. You haven't answered the most important question." She gave me another week to figure it out.

The following week I returned to Joyce's house and handed her my homework. Without opening it, she asked, "What'd you learn?"

"My purpose in life is to help God build His kingdom here on Earth," I replied.

"How are you going to do that?" *She's brutal . . .*

"I haven't a clue. My gift is teaching. Granted, I read passages in the Bible every day as part of my morning ritual, but I am certainly *not* equipped to teach it! Moreover, I have no intention of ever going to seminary, nor do I have the desire to do so. So, I don't know. I'm not exactly sure I've done the homework correctly," I said.

"You have," said Joyce. "Now let's talk about how you're

going to strategically reach the life you've envisioned while building God's kingdom, as you say."

Over the years, my purpose statement evolved into a statement that easily rolls off my tongue. My life purpose is to engage, equip, and empower individuals and organizations to overcome obstacles and create their best future in a context of love, joy, peace, and gratitude, and in harmony with the greatest good of all concerned.

It's nice, neat, and succinct. Notice, if you will, what's missing.

My intention here is to not get all preachy and teachy about God and country, and I promise you I won't. But here's the kicker. I've been leaving God out of many of my decisions. Yeah, so? I've been wanting to leave this desert. Every time I have decided to leave here, on the day of my planned departure, some tragedy occurs. Coincidence? I'm not sure, but I'm thinking about it. Every crisis. Every four months. So, let's look at the following statement for a moment.

"And we know that in all things God works for the good of those who love him, who have been called according to *his purpose*." (Romans 8:28 NIV, emphasis added).

Four months before being diagnosed with celiac disease, and not knowing if I would be alive for much longer (I had dropped twenty pounds within a two-week period and my body wasn't absorbing anything), I plowed ahead and opened my private consulting practice in late March 2015, signed a one-year lease, and established my business in the most magnificent corner office space overlooking the plaza of the resort community in which I was living. My health was not up to speed, but I didn't care at that point. *I'm not a victim, I'm a victor!* I was happy and ready to fulfill my vision-driven future, and nothing aside from death was going to stop me . . . until it did.

It's been seven years, and somewhere in the middle of it, I noticed a pattern of every four months something catastrophic occurring. *Interesting.* So, before randomly opening my Bible this morning, the following thoughts surfaced: *Why can't I write this chapter on hope? It shouldn't be this difficult. What is it about every four months that something unexpected shows up . . . like clockwork? What am I missing? What do I need to know?*

I opened my Bible to the book of Job 42. From the notes section: "Don't draw inward from the pain. Proclaim your faith in God, know that he cares . . ."

Am I being prepared for a special service, learning to be compassionate to those who suffer? Hmmm? Go back to Romans 8:28 . . . review your life's purpose statement, the original one you wrote down with Joyce. Why here, in Tucson? Why am I not able to leave? THINK! I don't have the skills it takes to help God. Up until now . . . Do what you can with what you have from where you are.

It's been four months since I moved out of my beautiful home into a small apartment overlooking the Catalina Mountains. Each morning I open the sliding glass door and listen to the trickling sounds of the water feature on the patio, the birds sing morning songs to one another, and I feel the cool, soft breeze coming through the door onto my face, watching God's glory as the sun rises over the mountain. Morgan, who has adjusted to her new surroundings, lovingly lays at my feel. I've never been happier than I am right now. It's been an exceptionally long and arduous journey to get here. The mountain on which I live gives me peace, and the name of this mountain puts a smile on my lips. It's known as Dove Mountain, and it reminds me that I feel so blessed for all the challenges that are behind me.

Just like Dorothy, Scarecrow, Tinman, and Lion in the *Wizard of Oz* who are traveling along the yellow brick road full of hope in finding true meaning and some gold, I too have been traveling this same yellow road for seventy-three years now, but we're never too old. There are plenty of gold nuggets that are ours for the asking to have and to hold.

My hope is found in my God's love. I am convinced now that things don't happen to me, they happen *for* me. I am struck by the number of pieces in the entire scheme of things that need to get put in place to ensure we're at the right place at the right time to do the work we are called to do.

As I have mentioned several times already, I am a teacher. I see my job as being a tour guide of sorts across open terrain. My job is not to convince you to think the same thoughts I think, or believe in a certain way, or load you up with "should" or "ought." It is to encourage exploration and a willingness to examine something through a different lens.

I have never, up until now, been able to figure out how I am to help God build His kingdom. Up until now, I have silenced my voice about my faith in God, because mention of Him is offensive to some. So, I had to ask myself, "Why is that?" I used to be an eye-roller whenever I heard anyone saying, "God told me to x, y, or z this morning." Or "I've been called to do missionary work." *Really?*

And then one day I accidentally walked into a church where it was as though God Himself was addressing me. Every word out of the speaker's mouth pierced my soul. *Wow. I've never known a God like that one.* I got curious, so week after week I went back to the church, and week after week I had the same experience. *Hello, God, thank you for your message. Would you mind talking with the rest of the people here today please. I'm feeling embarrassed about taking all of your time. Amen.* Every Sunday for months and months, God seemed to know exactly what I needed to hear. And to think that I happened on that church one day by taking a wrong turn on a morning I felt my most broken. It's a God thing.

I share this with you to let you know what I've been able to experience, simply by being open. If you find yourself experiencing recurring crises, or if you ever feel a tug at your heartstring and need to find someone who you can count on, consider taking it up in conversation with God, especially if you are not getting the results you need from others.

I am a spiritual being who happens to believe God the Father, the Son, and Holy Spirit are my higher power, and I boldly profess it. Don't let your past experiences, church, political affiliation, or political correctness, etc., blind you from moving forward (reconnecting) with God on a whole new level. He accepts us and welcomes us right where are. I know this to be true. I've been traveling this road searching for hope for a long, long time, and learned years ago that my hope is found in Him.

My message is solely one of my sources of hope. I am a servant. I am a writer. I am a speaker, a teacher, and a trainer. My name is Laurel Joakimides.

May the Lord bless you, and keep you, make His face shine upon you, and be gracious to you and your children, and their children, and their children . . . Amen.

ABOUT LAUREL JOAKIMIDES

Laurel Joakimides is a #1 international best-selling author, transformational speaker and trainer, and assistant producer of Dr. Angela Sadler-Williamson's documentary series: *Authentic Conversations.* As a certified Canfield trainer in the Success Principles, and a Strategic Futuring facilitator, Laurel is passionate about offering individuals and organizations dynamic programs to help them overcome obstacles and create their best future.

For more than twenty years, Laurel enjoyed working in high-tech companies throughout Silicon Valley and Santa Cruz, California. Upon completion of her master's program in 1995, she began her teaching career as an adjunct professor in the Department of Communication Studies at San Jose State University, California. Over the course of sixteen years, Laurel lectured at five universities and community colleges throughout the San Francisco Bay Area in California and Klamath Falls, Oregon, where she specialized in teaching critical decision-making in small groups, interpersonal communication, public speaking, and listening. Together with a colleague, she created and conducted servant leadership training and development programs for both profit and non-profit organizations. In 2014, a series of setbacks helped ignite her career as a multifarious entrepreneur with a passion to serve and help others find their voice.

Facebook: www.facebook.com/laureljoakimides.31
Facebook Fan Page: @LaurelsVisionDrivenLife
Email: laurel@laureljoakimides.com
www.laureljoakimides.com

CREATE WHAT YOUR HEART DESIRES

Tara LePera

"'For I know the plans I have for you,' declares the Lord, 'plans to prosper you and not to harm you, plans to give you hope and a future.'"

—Jeremiah 29:11 NIV

Everything we experience in life has a place in helping us develop the unique purpose we are each created for. Our purpose is preordained. We may not know what our own unique purpose in the universe is, but if we listen and watch for the lessons to be learned, *our purpose will be revealed.*

Have you ever sat and thought to yourself, "How will I be remembered when I'm gone? Will I leave an everlasting impact on my children, husband, family, friends, and even strangers I've met?" It has been said that we have two dates attached to us, the date we enter this world and the date we leave this world. The most important lesson is that we can create our own unique timelines alongside our faith in God, the Universe, or whatever spiritual force you are aligned with. Once we are born, we become part of our parents' or guardians' journey, and they play an essential role in our mental, physical, and emotional development. Later in life, we start to discover our own personal interests regarding work, relationships, social connections, etc. This can make a person start to feel like a chameleon adapting to all life's scenarios and learning lessons from experiences along the way.

What follows are some personal lessons I have learned that I would like to share with you. Our experiences at every phase of our lives, both bad and good, help to make us unique. I hope what I share throughout my story will give you strength on your life journey.

My Early Years

Alongside my parents' journey, we moved around a lot. I don't remember very much from these years, but I can strongly remember the fights my parents would get into and how it would affect me at the time. I can recall the day I looked up at my mom after one of their arguments and said, "I'm sorry Daddy is a jerk. Why don't you just leave him?" In that moment I believe I gave my mom that extra bit of courage she needed to follow her heart. My dad wasn't a bad guy; it was just clear they grew apart. It's crazy to think at such a young age I wanted nothing more than my parents to separate. I didn't realize the lesson until I got older. I now know that the lesson is that we don't ever have to stay in a situation we aren't happy in, especially if it's beyond broken. If God closes a door, it's for a reason.

My Teenage Years

My teenage years were a dark decade for me, but I believe it made me who I am. My parents separated and we were living with my mom. I started hanging out with a rebellious group of friends. Since my mom was always working and barely home, someone called child protective services on us. I remember the knock on our door that day so clearly. My younger sister and I were placed in a few different homes, and my brother was sent to a center just for boys. We were there a little over four months, but it seemed like an eternity. My mom and her boyfriend at the time, Lance, did everything they were told to do to get us back.

Towards the end of seventh grade, we moved and I was living in yet another town, hours away from my friends. I started to question myself: "Who am I? Will I fit in?" I developed low self-esteem and was not very optimistic about this new move.

As time went on, I ended up meeting some amazing friends; especially my two best friends Kristy and Jeremy.

Entering high school, I struggled a lot with paying attention. Learning didn't come easy for me when it seemed to for my peers. I was placed in special education classes and felt embarrassed. I did not want to show my face in school. Masking these feelings, I began drinking and smoking marijuana, which pushed me back even more. I began to not show up and eventually dropped out of high school the summer before eleventh grade and was introduced to the dancing scene. It wasn't where I expected to wind up, but at the time, I was having fun and making the money that I needed to help support my family.

Around this time, my best friend Jeremy was diagnosed with Non-Hodgkin's lymphoma. I didn't understand cancer at the time or how it was going to affect Jeremy. It was heartbreaking to watch him fight this at such a young age. Sadly, he lost his battle days before his twenty-first birthday. I was empty inside and started to experience anxiety for the first time at the age of nineteen and fell into a dark place. I knew I had to get out of this head space but didn't know where to start.

Looking back, I see it took me a while to release the anger I held onto during this time, but I am now grateful for the lessons I learned, the people God placed in my life during this time, and the strength I had at such a young age.

My Reveling Twenties

I found out I was pregnant from a guy I was seeing at the time. I was excited but nervous because I was unsure of how he'd react. He immediately offered me money for an abortion and said to not ever contact him again. It is crazy to think back and realize how verbally abusive he was. He would tell me nobody would want me since I was going to be a single mom and dancer. I allowed his words to affect me for a while, but I knew I deserved more, especially since I was about to be a new mom. I felt alone and needed a way to express my feelings. I started to journal for the first time, and it was amazing how it helped me throughout my pregnancy. It is clear that God gifted me with Alessia for me and only me, not her dad. He created me to be a strong woman, and Alessia was going to make me even stronger.

After having Alessia at age twenty-one, my anxiety became worse, and then 9/11 happening. I was terrified to go outside and leave the house. What was going on with me? I could barely sleep or eat and went down to 99 lbs. I definitely know it was the stress of bringing a new life into this world by myself on top of postpartum depression and anxiety. I was not familiar with what postpartum was or why I was feeling that way. I eventually went to see a doctor to get on an antidepressant, and it helped greatly over the next few years. I strongly felt the next step for me would be to quit dancing, so I started bartending until I eventually entered the corporate world at twenty-six. Here I am finally with a real big-girl job, yet I still felt out of place. I was working/traveling a lot. I was able to save up enough money over the next three years and purchase my first home right before my thirtieth birthday. It was an incredible accomplishment to be able to give my daughter Alessia and I a place of our own.

As I look back, although I was ashamed of my past for many years, I now see the clarity in it all. Regardless of any circumstances in our past, it does not dictate who we are today. Continue to rise up and only look back to see how far you have come.

Terrific Thirties

"Okay, this is it. I'm thirty years old. This is the age life is all supposed to start falling into place, right?" I had the career, a house, and the guy I was dating at the time eventually moved in. A year later, he asked me to marry him. I knew it was coming, but I did everything I could that day to dodge it. I knew over time he wasn't the one for me, especially since he was extremely toxic and would constantly accuse me of cheating when he was the one doing it. It took me a year, but I finally got him out of our life. It was the best thing I ever did.

I don't regret past relationships because they showed me who I didn't want to be when I was with them. It gave me the direction I needed at the time. I'm grateful God gave me the signs I needed to move on. When God wants to remove someone from your life, let him. Sometimes the exact people we fight to keep in our presence are the ones hurting us the most. Although I was moving in the right direction, I still struggled with my body image and a poor self-perception.

As a young girl I lacked self-love, confidence, and struggled with my body image. Being four eleven with a smaller figure always made me feel like a little girl. I felt the need to bring my confidence back more after my breakup. At age thirty-two, I decided to get breast enhancement surgery. At the time, it gave me the confidence I thought I needed, and not to mention I finally felt like a woman, not a girl.

During those years, my alcohol consumption was increasing again and I felt lost within. I knew this wasn't the path I wanted, especially after everything I worked so hard for. I felt God nudging at me to start digging deep within to find who I wanted to be. That's exactly what I did. I started to do things for me.

I started being more open and paid attention to who God wanted to place in my life. After months of focusing on myself and my daughter, on December 18, 2011, I went to an Eagles game with the seats that would change my life forever. God's plan of divine timing guided me to the person that would eventually be my life partner, my husband, Marc. He was different from anyone I had ever met before. The walls that I had built up were coming down, and I let him into my and Alessia's life.

My past showed up a lot in the beginning of our relationship and almost caused me to lose Marc forever, but once again, God showed up and guided me to release my old feelings and patterns from my previous relationships to begin this new journey. I had to stop drinking, stop sabotaging myself. I had to learn to have trust for once in my life, especially if I wanted a future with Marc. I did a complete one-eighty, and my new lifestyle included working out, starting our health and wellness journey, and leaving my miserable nine to five corporate job. I felt that this was finally my new beginning that I have always wanted. I even went on and completed my GED at age thirty-five.

October 31, 2013, Marc and I participated in a Halloween urban scramble run in Philadelphia. When the run was over, Marc had gotten down on one knee and asked me to marry him. I was in awe, and even better, Philadelphia magazine was there to capture it all. Nine months later, I married my best friend, and we couldn't wait to start expanding our family and life together. Six months later, we found out we were pregnant. Now expanding our family, we decided to list our home in Pennsylvania and purchased a new home in NJ. It was definitely a sad moment since we had created so many incredible memories in that house. The move was hard on all of us, but it took Alessia more time to adapt, moving during her high school years. As a mom, it crushed me to see her struggling, especially since I knew how she was feeling. She did eventually find some great friends that helped her with the transition and knowing her baby sister was on her way.

On September 20, 2015, RaeLynn Jane LePera was born. Alessia was finally a big sister, and we were all thrilled. I finally felt like everything was falling into place, but I started noticing signs of postpartum depression and anxiety again. I ignored the signs and convinced myself maybe it was something else. I didn't want to fill my body with antidepressants again. I immediately started becoming more active in my workout routine, and man, did it help me get through those off-balance and dark days. I even threw myself into more self-development sessions and attended coaching classes/programs. During this time, I met some remarkable people who I learned from along the way. I highly recommend surrounding yourself with motivational and uplifting people. Speaking of supportive people, Marc was my number one supporter during the next few years of building myself up, and I honestly would not be here today sharing most of this with you if I didn't have his support. I started to connect the messages and signs God was trying to show me during the time I was working on myself. It wasn't all about me; it was about the women he brought into my life who I needed to uplift and support in believing in themselves. He guided me through my healing and growth to build up others.

There is something about making an emotional and uplifting connection when working with someone. We get so much more out of our life when we stop making it all about ourselves. It changes the way we show up in the world, and life will reward us and continue to do so. In 2016, I slowly started to build my self-love and success business. On May 7, 2018, my dad contacted us letting us know that my half-sister, Hope, had just given birth to a baby boy, but child services were stepping in. The baby was born addicted to drugs, and he was going to be another victim of the foster care system. Having been through foster care myself, I could not imagine allowing one of my family members to experience what I had to go through, so we agreed to take him. This is when our son Charlie came into our lives. Little did we know how this little boy would bring so much joy and happiness into our lives. However, having a neonatal abstinence syndrome baby comes with some major struggles. Charlie had to go through withdrawal from all the drugs. There were many sleepless nights, tons of tears and anger, but Charlie was progressing each day.

Looking back, the lesson of this decade was to not limit myself, to let go of control and trust that God knows our journey before we do. He has given me the strength to push through things when I didn't believe in myself.

Self-Love Forties

A few months after I turned forty, we found out we were pregnant again. We were trying for another baby before we found out about Charlie, but put it off for a while and said, "If it happens, it's meant to be." So there we were, raising our daughters, helping our son heal, getting ready for the birth of another child, all while building our marriage. Relationships are tested often, but through these tests, ours was strengthened for sure. We welcomed our son Hudson William LePera into the world a month early but healthy as can be. Even though I was now a mother of four, I still stayed true to myself. I attended uplifting events and gave as much self-love I needed to show up for my babies, even with all the daily craziness.

My friend Penelope invited me to a Dare to Dream publisher's event hosted by Kate Butler. I always knew in my heart I would share my story in a book someday, but I was always afraid of judgment. As I was walking into the event, I turned the corner and there was a banner staring right at me with lights shining down from above. "This is your time, Tara." I just knew this was my sign. I walked into that event feeling so inspired and ready, and that same day I signed up to co-author my first book, *Women Who Rise*. By far one of the best experiences I ever had other than giving birth to my babies. I always say, "Our story is never too broken to help others rise up. God will take our broken things and turn them into beautiful things," and he sure did.

A few months later, Marc was offered a new position within the government. Instead of it being located in New Jersey, it was located in Arizona. Marc and I have been manifesting to move to Arizona since 2014. His previous job at the time took him away for days/weeks at a time, and he wanted to be home more helping to raise the kids. This new job was going to be able to provide that for us. Now it was my time to step up and support my husband in following his dreams as he has always done for me. We had to break the news to our family and friends that we would be moving across the country. It definitely wasn't easy! Crazy enough, we were beyond ready for the new journey ahead. We had some stressful times getting the house ready to be listed; there was so much to be done in such little time. Then our world turned upside down when COVID hit. My anxiety was creeping back in, but I did my best to keep it together for my family. I was on a roller coaster of emotions.

May 7, 2020 was launch day for *Women Who Rise*! The book was released, and we became a #1 best-seller in fifteen categories and best-seller in twenty-six categories. Wild, right? Once my story was out into the world, this is when my self-love coaching business started to grow. I stopped allowing fear to get in the way of what your heart always desired.

Then, life got even better. On June 23, 2020, our adoption with Charlie (over Zoom) was finalized; he is officially a LePera. COVID wasn't holding us back; life must still go on. Then before we knew it, our moving date was here. We loaded up in our RV and headed toward our new hometown state of Arizona. This was one of the most exciting and unknown experiences yet as a family. The cross-country road trip was amazing. I have to be honest, even though I was excited for the move and my husband's new career, I was still struggling with anxiety and postpartum depression. It started to affect me even more, especially knowing Marc was leaving for the Academy for seven months in New Mexico. We did not know if we would be able to see him due to COVID restrictions. Right before Marc left, I lost my Nana to COVID, and a few days later, my Uncle Louis as well. Here I was with my kids in a new place, with only my best friend Kristy in the next town over, missing my family.

The first year here in Arizona was by far my darkest year. At moments, I was weak and had scary, intrusive thoughts to the point I thought I was going crazy. This isn't me! Who was I becoming? I would cry myself to bed almost every night, praying and asking God to heal me. I would sit and wonder if what I was experiencing could be depression, postpartum, menopause, my breast implant illness, a nervous breakdown, or everything all at once? I was very open the entire time with how I was feeling with Marc, Kristy, a few close friends back in NJ, and especially my daughter Alessia. I can't thank her enough for helping me while Marc was away. She was honestly my rock. I knew Marc was nervous to leave us for the Academy for sure, but I knew I was going to pull through and show up and be the best mom that I know I could be. So, I did just that. I put my coaching business on hold for over a year and dedicated all my time to the kids and making our new house a home so when Marc was done with the Academy he would come home and feel complete.

Sometimes our world can come crashing down, and we have no answers to why it is happening to us, and it can be terrifying. But I know in my heart God created me to be a strong woman. He would never throw something I couldn't handle my way. I have to say I am truly grateful for how my faith has continued to grow throughout my life, especially these past two years. I have since found some amazing friends here in Arizona, and I honestly don't know what I would do without them. Marc came home from the Academy on July 15, 2021, and life has been falling into place.

I'm also happy to share that almost a year later, I had my breast implants removed, and I feel like I'm back home in my body. I'm grateful to be on the healing journey now. I also just recently started my self-love and success coaching business back up, and I feel so complete working with these remarkable women. This September will be two years since we moved here to Arizona, and I honestly can say I wouldn't change anything. We absolutely love it here.

My lesson learned so far is God is still writing my story. I won't let go of my faith because of what I have yet to see. I know everything I've been through was to give me the strength and wisdom I required to be where I am today. No matter what we have been through in life, we still have the ability to create what our heart desires. So stop allowing your past to dictate your future so our purpose can be revealed.

To my children, Alessia, RaeLynn, Charlie, and Hudson. Remember the most important relationship you will have in life is the one you will have with yourself. No matter what you will ever go through in life, trust that God is in the details, and he already knows the plans for you. There will always be beautiful new adventures ahead, and you have the ability to create them.

To my husband, Marc, thank you for always uplifting and believing in me. I'm truly grateful for the adventurous life we have created together. I can't wait to see what else God has ahead for all of us.

Some of Gods greatest gifts are unanswered prayers!

ABOUT TARA LEPERA

Tara Ann LePera is the founder of Self Love and Success, a self-love coach, a manifesting mama, a motivational speaker, a #1 best-selling co-author of *Women Who Rise* and created her own self-love and manifesting journal.

For the last seven years, Tara has focused her expertise on personal development, growing her self-love, building a strong mindset, and learning how to manifest her dreams into reality.

While growing up, Tara lacked confidence and viewed herself in a negative way. It wasn't until Tara learned to tap into her inner-most truth and shift her limiting beliefs in her capabilities that she launched herself in alignment and co-created a life and business that makes her proud.

Tara's primary focus and joy is working with women. Her main focus is teaching multiple self-love techniques in order to build confidence while sparking the inner energy back into their lives. Tara does this through one-on-one coaching, group support systems, as well as programs and courses that are focused on professional life development, self-love, manifestation, confidence, and resetting.

Tara is the mother of four children and married to her husband, Marc. Tara and her family live in Maricopa, Arizona, and love to explore the world together while living life to its fullest, all while creating everlasting memories.

Tara welcomes you to connect with her by visiting

www.selfloveandsuccess.com
Email: Taraannlepera@gmail.com
Instagram: @selfloveandsuccess and @Tara_LePera
Facebook: Tara Ann LePera
TikTok: @taralepera827

THE EDUCATOR'S EDGE: ASK! ASK! ASK!

Denise McCormick, M.A.E.

What does it mean to lead with legacy? When someone dies, they are remembered by many people, and that becomes their legacy. At age thirteen, I was golfing beside my friend Kathy when she was struck in the head by a golf ball. The next day, she died of a brain hemorrhage. Upon learning of her death, I decided to lead my own life with legacy by making positive choices in my life. It was very comforting to me after Kathy was gone that a part of her remained with me beyond the memories we shared together. Her achieving spirit and lofty goals in life inspired me to set big goals, and then believe I could achieve them. I am so grateful for the gift of Kathy's legacy inspired my own.

One Legacy Story

What are you saying to yourself?

Do you ever stop and ask yourself that question? What are you saying to yourself?

WHAT YOU SAY TO YOUR MIND,
YOUR MIND THEN SAYS TO YOU.
IT ALL STARTS WITH YOUR WORDS,
WHICH YOU HAVE THE POWER TO CHOOSE.

I had to stop and ask myself that question: *What am I saying to myself?*

Fourteen years ago, I was a third-grade teacher struggling to breathe. I'll get to that in a moment, but first let me give you some background.

For twenty-six years, I taught elementary, university, and graduate school students. Like all of you reading this today, I too share a deep love of supporting our children.

Children are the seeds of the future, and as educators, we are like the fertile soil in which these seeds are cultivated and encouraged to grow. You never know what you will get—what that child will develop into—but watching the miracle of that unique growth in every child is truly the deepest joy in our work as teachers.

In the best-selling book, *Women Who Shine,* I share the following quote: "We as educators plant seeds in the mind to shine with our belief in the child's ability, which then illuminates that child's world for a lifetime! What an incredible miracle and responsibility we are entrusted with, shining the light of belief on the genius of a child!"[1]

As a third-grade teacher in Iowa, I began to see that the fertile soil within me as an educator was becoming less and less fertile. In fact, I was struggling to breathe. I was *not* getting what I personally needed to function, let alone thrive as an educator to be able to then give my best to the students. As a world traveler, every time I have flown, they give the safety instructions to put your own oxygen mask on first so you will be able to help others. And I needed to put on my oxygen mask to breathe in my classroom. It was going to be up to me!

It started with a sinus infection, that turned into another . . . and then another.

For eight years, I stayed in this third-grade classroom, sick from chronic sinus infections and my immune system hampered

---

1—Denise McCormick, *Women Who Shine* (Kate Butler Books, 2021).

by countless rounds of antibiotics. It became clear that something in this classroom was making me sick. At the urging of our daughter, a pediatrician in Australia, I finally went to an allergist and got tested. Turns out I was allergic to two kinds of dust mites! My allergist told me I needed to be in a room with air conditioning and no carpet. With a second signed recommendation for air conditioning for my health, I planned my strategy for continuing to secure a classroom in which I could breathe.

First I asked the school administration to transfer me to an opening in an air-conditioned building. That first request was denied. I then went along with the teachers' rights advocate to question that decision, as I had the contractual right to do so. Denied again.

So I went to another meeting, told them my situation again, and showed them two doctors that had written recommendations for air conditioning to be installed in my classroom so I could breathe and be healthy. (I even offered to pay for the air conditioner). This request too was denied. I was told, "Maybe we should just move you to somewhere where you didn't have that problem."

I stood up, feeling angry, but I contained my composure and quietly shared with them, "You'll be hearing from my lawyer." I then slipped out of the room.

It hit me hard as I walked out of that meeting: my health and well-being were *not* a priority for the school administration, and no one was going to change this but me! I knew I needed to look first at my own thinking on this entire situation, so I sat myself down and had a real talking-to with myself. I remembered in that moment an essential truth:

WHAT YOU SAY TO YOUR MIND,
YOUR MIND THEN SAYS TO YOU.
IT ALL STARTS WITH YOUR WORDS,
WHICH YOU HAVE THE POWER TO CHOOSE.

So, I asked myself, *What am I saying to myself? What am I saying to myself that is perpetuating this situation?* I realized I was saying things to myself that were keeping me stuck in the loop of staying in this sick classroom . . . for years! I advocated along with a community committee to have all the elementary buildings be air conditioned since the middle school and high school already were. Since the results were unsuccessful, I needed to change the story I was telling myself about what was possible and what I deserved.

A fire rose within me. I said to myself, "I have the right to breathe in my classroom!" I felt it! And I believed it: My right to be healthy. My right to matter. My right to have what I need so I can thrive—as a teacher, as a person.

This was the beginning of me developing a growth mindset in this situation. Bolstered by the belief that I had a right to thrive, a right to breathe in my own classroom, I set out to take steps to do what I needed to do to make sure I got what I needed.

After that, I got my allergist to write a recommendation for air conditioning and no carpeting. My lawyer began the long year-and-a-half process of negotiating with the school district's lawyer and ultimately the school board.

I had finally used my voice and believed I could make a difference.

Because I knew that this change would not happen overnight, I needed to ease my allergies *now*. I walked into my classroom and went over to the wall that was carpeted (yes, I said a carpeted wall) and ripped it off the wall. I was going to take action and ask for forgiveness later! And my health got a little better after that as they also removed the carpeting from the floor.

I spoke up, but when my requests for help were denied over and over. I was not going to simply stand there and continue to suffer. I took matters into my own hands and found the strength to do what I needed to do to take care of myself until the legal process could be completed. They first tried a dehumidifier and that made no difference. Finally, the school board intervened, and I was asked to pay for the air conditioner, and they would pay for the installation. I could take it with me when I retired, which I did.

That next fall, I had an air conditioner installed for my last two years of teaching. The principal announced to me that all the children with allergies and asthma had been placed in my room that fall. I smiled knowing that I was not the only one that would now be able to breathe and would no longer have to work in sweat shop conditions.

And wouldn't you know it! The following year, the school replaced all the old carpet and took measures to start conversations about air conditioning in the elementaries.

Many nights, I cried myself to sleep during the legal process. Every day though, I looked up at that wall and visualized the air conditioner keeping me and my students healthy and breathing freely, and I marched on!

Today, all the elementaries are air conditioned, and as I traveled to each to share my #1 international best-selling book, *Never Mind the Monkey Mind*, I rejoiced in the knowledge that by standing up for my right to breathe in my classroom, now all of the elementary classrooms had that right!

What Teachers Face Every Day / Diamond Insight

I share this story with you because this experience was an initiation into understanding—based on research—the many challenges teachers face every day:

- inspiring students to be more self-directed

- improving learning outcomes

- differentiating and personalizing teaching

- getting students to do their work outside the classroom

- securing safety on school campuses

- finding the time to keep up with administrative tasks

- understanding changing technology

- parental involvement

- teachers who are overworked

- teachers who spend out of their own pocket for school supplies the school does not provide

- teachers who do not get enough rest and self-care

Most people don't even consider the fact that teachers need to take care of themselves and grow in the personal understanding of themselves as a very valuable educator. The reality is that teachers do not get support for self-care or personal development anywhere in their teacher education training or in their professional development as teachers. If they did, there would be happier, healthier teachers with more energy to educate and less burnout. They would then be able to bring their best for their children's education.

A recent poll from the National Education Association in January helps quantify the stress being placed on educators right now as reported on NPR. Teachers are picking up the slack for absent colleagues and are covering unfilled positions. Fifty-five percent of them say they will leave teaching sooner than they had originally planned.[2]

Becky Pringle, president of the National Education Association, which has more than three million members, talks about the impetus of the survey: "Without exception, every stop I made, from Kentucky to Oakland, I heard similar stories of educators who were exhausted, overwhelmed, feeling unloved, disrespected."[3]

2—Alissa Alteri Shea, "Teachers say they don't feel supported. But what does authentic, genuine support look like?" Truth for Teachers, June 22, 2022, https://truthforteachers.com/what-does-authentic-support-for-teachers-look-like/.

3—Shea, "Teachers say they don't feel supported."

Other findings:[4]

- 90% of its members say that feeling burned-out is a serious problem.

- 86% say that they have seen more educators leaving the profession or retiring early since the start of the pandemic.

- 80% report that unfilled job openings have led to more work obligations for those left.

By facing the reality of this data, our voices need to be heard. While it may be uncomfortable, we must.

While it may seem daunting to speak up and use our voices, you must be uncomfortable even though you are exhausted with all that is already required of you!

Spirit and Growth Mindset

But here's what I want you to know: When you think you can't, when your mind says you can't, you are *not out of options*. At this point, your options have just opened up.

Iyanla Vanzant shares in her book, *Until Today,* the next time you face a challenge you believe you cannot handle, remember your personality is the passenger, not the driver! Your spirit is the driving force of your life. Most people believe it is the personality that matters. The reality is that as long as you insist on listening to the passenger, you will probably end up getting lost.[5]

The truth is that your spirit is the only true navigational force in your life. Unfortunately, it doesn't talk as loud as your personality. Your spirit offers directions only when asked. Your spirit, unlike your personality, is not so concerned with your comfort. It is concerned that you have a safe journey on the path of growth.

For some of you, what you need could be more pay. For

4—Shea, "Teachers say they don't feel supported."

5—Iyanla Vanzant, *Until Today!* (New York, NY: Atria, 2001).

others, it could be more support for resources for the classroom. For me, it was speaking up for my right to breathe.

In speaking up for what you need, you embark on the journey of having a growth mindset rather than a fixed mindset. With a growth mindset, you see your life as a series of challenges that you meet one by one, step by step, day by day. For each of these challenges, you must inquire, moment to moment, what are you saying to yourself?

What are the messages you are giving yourself?

Do they keep you down, or do they raise you up? Remember, your mind believes whatever you tell it!

After you have done the work to check and perhaps adjust what you are saying to yourself, what you believe about yourself and what you deserve, you speak up.

And every time you do, every time you speak up for what you stand for, you *grow*. You expand. You deepen. You heal. You powerfully create your life in a way that serves you and your ability to thrive.

Steps to Take Now

- What is it in your work as an educator right now where you are not getting what you need?

- What are you saying to yourself that is keeping you stuck in that dynamic?

- What can you say to yourself instead that honors what you need and your right to thrive?

- From this place, what do you need to say to those involved to honor this need and your right to thrive?

- What actions do you need to take?

Iyanla Vanzant says, "Women, you are preapproved by God. You don't need anyone's approval; you need to ask for support."[6]

Educators are the fertile soil in which the seeds of children's spirits and minds and hearts sprout and grow. Educators must be healthy and thriving if our children are to as well. Educators must stand for this truth, to develop powerful and healthy beliefs about the right to thrive, to speak up, and to lead from this place.

What keeps educators from doing this? For me, when I was stuck in that fixed mindset for eight years. I was telling myself a story about why I couldn't change the situation. I told myself things like, *But you're just an elementary teacher, I can't make this any better. Who am I to believe that I could have this when no one else has been able to?*

Those are stories. Were these stories really true? How do I know they're true? Where would I be if I didn't believe those stories? As educators, we can each choose to change the stories we tell ourselves about what is possible.

I decided to change what I said to myself and use a growth mindset. Instead of lack, I saw possibility. I started to visualize what my room would be like with that air conditioner on the wall—being able to breathe all day long, my students able to focus and work in an environment that served them and served me.

By using positive self-talk, educators will change the culture of the country's school system by recognizing and honoring their right to self-care and well-being. This will reignite for all educators their zest for teaching. This is The Educator's Edge.

All I know is that when you take the time to ask this life-changing question, *What are you saying to yourself?* you empower yourself. You allow yourself to believe that what you are *now* saying to yourself is important and possible. With that seed planted, you then go to work to water, fertilize, and weed your own garden day after day. You learn in that instance that you have the right to shine.

6—Vanzant, *Until Today!*

The challenge is to be strong enough to stand alone, smart enough to know when you need help, and brave enough to ask for it!

Planting seeds to shine in the mind takes deep fertile listening. Just ask the question, *What are you saying to yourself?* Then stay silent and listen. Notice that *silent* and *listen* are spelled with the same letters.

When I finally granted myself permission to be silent and listen, I asked my spirit, *What should I do?* I asked for support and so can you!

ABOUT DENISE MCCORMICK, M.A.E.

Denise McCormick, M.A.E. is the very definition of a growth mindset expert. At age thirteen, a tragic accident and loss of her friend inspired Denise to lead her own life with legacy. Denise is a state-awarded educator, #1 international best-selling author, inspirational speaker, and associate producer with Dr. Angela Sadler Williamson's PBS documentary series: *Authentic Conversations.* She is a certified Canfield trainer in the Success Principles, a licensed WomanSpeak Circle Leader and the CEO of Success Mindset Mentorship, LLC. As a former elementary educator, education lecturer, K–12 reading specialist at Iowa Wesleyan University, and Iowa Writing Project Instructor, Denise has over thirty years in education.

Denise's work as The Educator's Coach finds her coaching with individuals and groups. Her programs are on her created private Facebook page, The Educator's Edge. She is passionate about supporting educators around their self-care and personal development, areas she felt were lacking in her years of teaching elementary, university, and graduate school classrooms. She has written three books as an author of her first children's book, *Never Mind the Monkey Mind*; a featured author in *Women Who Impact;* and a legacy author in *Women Who Shine.*

You can connect with Denise at:

www.denisemccormick.com
Email: denise@denisemccormick.com
LinkedIn: www.linkedin.com/in/
denisemccormick-m-a-e-86484987
Instagram: @deniseamccormick

GROW THROUGH WHAT YOU GO THROUGH

Kristi Ann Pawlowski

Everyone has a different idea of what their legacy will be or what they will leave behind to their families when they are no longer physically here on earth. Some people are concerned with leaving their loved ones money, riches, family heirlooms, etc. Of course, my hope is to leave my children with some financial stability, but the greater gift I wish to leave behind are my words of wisdom. I have lots of advice to leave behind for sure, but my greatest wisdom that I hope to instill in them at a young age is that there is always a rainbow to find in/after every storm or difficult season. I also hope they learn self-love is important and doing what makes *you* happy is the most important thing in life.

I can remember from the time I was a young girl when a bad situation occurred in my life, it was taught as a negative situation—almost as if I was being punished by some being. *Why is this happening to me?!* I can still hear my mom's words echoing, "What are we supposed to do now?"

I am trying not to repeat this generational thinking. Instead, I want to instill in my children at a young age (so they don't have to take the forty-plus years I did to realize) to change the negative mindset and tone of that statement to "Why do I get to experience this?" and "What's next?!"

Here are some lessons I have learned in life that I hope will not only help my children but their children's children and anyone else reading this who needs to hear it!

Finding Your Rainbow of Self-Love

I went on vacation with my family to Mexico shortly after having COVID-19, so my beach body was less than ideal at the time. Everyone can appreciate this, I am sure, because COVID became the time of no gyms, Netflix marathons, and eating nonstop from boredom and cabin fever. Sound familiar? Okay, so with that in mind, envision this scenario: I was at the pool packed with lots of people playing Name That Tune with my family. After only a few beats were played, I knew the song. It was Whitney Houston's song "Nothing." I was proud of myself because I earned my family five points. I did not expect what was to come next.

The entertainment staff said to me," If you come up here on stage and sing it for us on the microphone, we will give your family an additional five points." I looked at my kids' smiling faces, and without any hesitation jumped up on the stage in my two-piece bathing suit with a post-COVID body ready to sing a Whitney Houston song. Of all the artists, it was a Whitney song. We're talking major difficulty level here. However, I got up there and sang with more confidence than I ever would have in my teenage years when I was as fit as a fiddle. I belted out the song and used expressions while I sang, and the whole pool cheered for me as well as my kids and husband.

When it was all, over my daughter turned to me and said, "Mom, you got up there and did not care at all."

I said, "Yes, Charlotte, that is right!"

She then said back, "Well, it's Mexico, Mom. You did not know anyone here anyway, so it did not matter. Right, Mom?"

I looked her intensely in the eyes and said, "Charlotte, I would not care if I knew everyone here, I still would have gotten up there and done that. Never worry about what anyone thinks. Do what makes *you* happy!"

In that moment, my goal of teaching them to have self-love and do what makes them happy was accomplished.

Finding Your Rainbow When Caring for a Terminally Ill Parent—My Father

My father had a rare form of cancer and was sick for about fifteen years on and off. He would receive treatment, go into remission, and then the cancer would spread to a different area that needed to be treated. This experience made me aware that I was stronger than I ever knew was possible. I learned that my faith in God helped me to recognize that my father was going to be in a better place where there was no suffering, sickness, or worry. He was going to be rejoicing in heaven with the Lord instead, and that gave me such peace and calmness throughout the whole process. My faith was evident to people around me because my trials displayed strength instead of weakness or despair.

Finding Your Rainbow When Caring for a Terminally Ill Parent—My Mother

My dad passed away in January 2020. My mom appeared perfectly healthy at the time. She had COVID-19 in 2021, so she seemed a bit tired, but nothing out of the ordinary. She went to the doctor because she was having trouble breathing. Again, we thought possible aftereffects of COVID-19, but it wasn't. They discovered a mass on her lung.

They did tests, and they revealed lung cancer. The doctor had to do more testing to see if she was a candidate for treatment, and of course, we were hoping for the best. The oncologist told us that immunotherapy was an option for treatment for my mother's lung cancer.

In the meantime, I had an appointment set up at another hospital with an oncologist who specialized in lung cancer. Their office called me in confusion. "Kristi, why is your mom coming to our office for an appointment this week for lung cancer when our pathology reports say she has breast cancer?"

What? "No, there must be some mistake!" Well, there was no mistake. By this time, my mom had a rare, fast-growing breast cancer that there was no cure for. It spread to her lung, sternum, bones in her back, etc. The pathologists misdiagnosed it because it was so rare. Within three weeks, she went from possibly being able to shrink the tumors and having up to two years to live, to their being absolutely no possibility of a cure.

She passed within days of us receiving this news.

Although my heart was broken, I felt at peace because I had a close, loving relationship with my mom while she was living and abided by her wishes of being in her home on hospice. The one thing that kept echoing with friends, nurses, and family members was "Look at the legacy she is leaving behind." Everyone had commented how my sister and I had been by her side this entire time. They all said, "You can tell she raised you well." I began to think my children were also learning a valuable lesson at a young age of six with my dad's passing and now eight with my mom's that caring for your parents is imperative, and I could only hope that they would learn through our example as we had learned through our mother's.

Finding Your Rainbow at Work

In my last book I wrote, *Woman Who Shine*, I shared that although I was devastated being moved to a new building in my school district, I knew there would be a new purpose. At the time, I felt heartbroken that I had to leave the kids I was currently working with and had worked with for many years as a speech/language pathologist.

However, as usual, God was moving me not only to protect me from harm that I was encountering in my former building, but he was opening new doors for me. Being moved to the high school led me to be with students I once worked with in pre-school and early elementary grades. I now got the opportunity to work with them again. I was able to see the part that I played in getting them to where they were now.

Students who I once provided therapy for, helped learn to read, and tutored were now mostly juniors and seniors and were getting ready to graduate and head to college. These students were now sharing their triumphs with me, and I got to be part of it. These students were passing driver's education, publishing books, becoming track stars, football stars, and were thriving. They were reaching their dreams and goals that they shared with me at a young age. Contributing to their success and seeing the amazing individuals they had become was heart-warming to say the least.

Moving to a new building gave me new responsibilities and challenges, which were also welcoming to me. My heart is so full here. I know I am where I am supposed to be. I love that student's stop by daily to see how my day is going. My other students remind me daily that I am a great teacher by the words and actions they convey.

Finding Your Rainbow in Relationships

1. Let go of certain expectations.

2. Social media is the devil.

3. When you forgive, you are more likely to forget the bad.

4. Ladies, when trying to find a man in your life, SEEK GOD FIRST!

5. You need to love yourself before anyone else can love you or you can love anyone else.

6. Find a partner who loves not just pieces of you but all of you. Love someone who loves you back unconditionally.

7. People cheat for different reasons. Most likely, *you* were not one of them.

8. Trust in God. Let him be in control of opening and closing doors for you. Trust in his plan; it is always better than your own!

9. Be with someone because they meet and exceed *your* expectations, not others'. Find someone that makes you happy!

10. I have learned that when people appear not to support you or side with you, it is not because they don't believe what you are saying is true, but they are too much of a coward to stand up and do what is right.

11. Do *not* let people's negative thoughts, actions, and words deter you from reaching your dreams and goals. Succeeding in life is the biggest f*** you back to them.

Finding Your Rainbow When You Least Expect it

I was driving with my daughter one day in the car. I had just recently recovered from my third time having COVID-19; two occurrences were less than ninety days apart. At that time, I was experiencing great fatigue. However, what was even worse was the brain fog I had developed from it. The brain fog was making me have memory loss, and for a short period of time, I thought I was possibly suffering from dementia. During this time, I had to rely on the memory strategies that I taught my students and clients. Using these strategies daily was not enough, and I really knew I could not fix this problem on my own. I quickly investigated who could assist me with this horrible brain fog and memory loss I was having. Who would help with such a task?

I already knew the answer to this . . . an SLP, of course! During my first therapy session, tears began to stream down my face. How could I possibly be a practicing speech language pathologist and need to receive services myself? How could such simple tasks be so hard for me? Here come those words again: *Why is this happening to me?!*

I not only connected with a fabulous SLP but learned even more strategies and resources that helped me *and* my students. Also, my empathy for my clients increased because I could literally feel their pain. What else positive could possibly come out of this? Well, hold onto your seat belt. I am about to tell you . . .

While driving my daughter to dance one night, my brain fog kicked in big time. I started driving her to tap class but had to stop at the music store first to fix my son's violin, which was in six pieces. I took a wrong turn and got frustrated with myself because we were on a time crunch. I turned the car around when I realized after five minutes that I was going the wrong way. I got to the music store ten minutes before it was closing, got him a new instrument, and we were on our way again! On the way to the dance studio, there was a horrific accident. My daughter looked out the left side of her window at the crashed cars, and what was about to come out of her mouth, I did not expect at all. She said, "See, Mom, God made you make the wrong turn to save us from being in that accident."

Tears began to roll down my face. I responded back to her by saying ,"Charlotte, you are *so* right. Isn't God good?" Ah. After I caught my breathe, I wanted to scream from the rooftops.

I taught her that. I taught her to turn a bad situation into a good one. I taught her—am teaching her daily—to find the rainbow in her storms . . . not just this one we encountered, but for any she faces in the future.

When I first began trusting in God and surrendering my worries to him, I found my purpose in life. It taught me how to see things in a different light. I hope my knowledge and light is not only poured out to my own children, but my children's children. I hope the legacy I leave behind of growing through the pain as you go through the pain and finding the rainbows in your storms will help continue to build strength, hope, and positivity for this generation and many that follow.

Channing and Charlotte, I dedicate the following chapter to you. I can't wait to see "What's next!" in your life.

I also dedicate this chapter to my beautiful mother Victoria Pawlowski who passed away while writing this book on July 21, 2022. Her legacy was making a positive difference in people's lives and her extremely generous heart. She reminded us daily to do all things with a happy heart!

Love you more, Mom. (Squeeze, squeeze) xoxo

ABOUT KRISTI ANN PAWLOWSKI

Kristi Ann Pawlowski has worked in the field of education for twenty-three years as a speech language pathologist, and kindergarten and first-grade teacher. She has also taught classes at local colleges and universities, was an early intervention provider, and worked in the hospital setting as well. Kristi has an extensive background in performing arts and encourages others to find their true passion and purpose in life. Kristi's passion is helping people discover that "negative" things or difficult seasons that are occurring in their lives aren't really negative, but possibly gifts from God that have not been discovered yet.

Kristi helps people see the rainbow in their past and present storms through her workshops, Facebook page, and personal coaching. Kristi writes books that encourage kindness, promote empathy, and motivate others. Kristi is a #1 international best-selling author of the Inspired Impact Series *Women Who Empower* and *Women Who Shine*. She is also a two-time international best-selling children's author of her books *Differently-Abled Mable* and *Can a Leopard Change Its Spots?* She has a true desire to make a positive difference in the lives of adults and children. Kristi resides in New Jersey with her two beautiful children and her husband, Jason.

They say good things happen to good people. However, Kristi believes that unfortunate things happen to good people to make them better human beings.

To connect with Kristi, visit her Facebook page "Find Your Rainbow in the Storm" or connect with her via email at speechkp@yahoo.com.

LESSONS FROM MY CATS: TRUST, LISTEN, SURRENDER

Michelle A. Reinglass

I turned around for one more good-bye as the door closed behind her. Then I crawled into my car and cried. Mollie, one of my two beloved cats, would remain for three nights, four days at a specialty veterinary office for a medical procedure called radio-iodine. This treatment, for hyperthyroidism, entails injecting a cat with massive doses of iodine and radiation. She needed to stay there to allow some of the radiation to dissipate. The facility had set up a camera for those four days, which allowed me to see Mollie until "lights out" each night. I talked to her through the window, but of course she couldn't hear.

Mollie, along with her brother Oliver, grabbed my heart thirteen years earlier, at our farmers market. That was August 2008, during the Olympics. It was a usual Saturday morning at breakfast with my running buddies, following our weekly six-mile run. The conversation was about the Olympics. At some point, my mind took a trip down memory lane to an earlier Olympic year, 1984, when another cat appeared in my life.

I've been an avid runner for decades and belonged to two running groups. These were serious runners doing long-distance races including marathons and beyond. I ran my first marathon, the Women's Avon Marathon with this group.

This was 1983, and we were celebrating the upcoming '84 Olympics, which would debut the first women's marathon to be held during the Olympics. We were also excited to be running the Olympic marathon course with a grand finish in the Los Angeles Coliseum!

Members of the running group bought tickets for some of the track and field events, including the women's marathon. We were watching history, but we didn't know that in a few days, another historic event would happen in the women's 3,000-meter race.

There was big buzz about two Olympic runners, Mary Decker Slaney, favored to win, and the last-minute entry for Zola Budd, the "barefoot runner" from South Africa. That buzz became a "shout across the bow" when the two of them collided during the race. This race was already controversial because of the Olympic ban on South African athletes, due to apartheid.

Then, the collision happened. Either Zola stepped on Mary's shoe, or Mary's shoe stepped on Zola's bare foot. It was deemed too close to call, but the accusations by Mary against Zola were fast and furious. It was then that I anointed Zola Budd the underdog, my heroine, and stood up for her in many debates about the incident.

This is where the cat comes in. Soon after the collision, on a Sunday night, there was a knock at my door. There stood two friends from my running group. They had been at a garage sale and brought me a surprise! Loi, my marathon idol and mentor, had her hands behind her back, until a tiny, fluffy ball of peach and gray fur whizzed by me and upstairs to the den. I ran upstairs and found the kitten . . . inside my Nike running shoe. Not only that, she had turned herself around so her tiny head was resting on the back of the shoe. My protestations dissolved seeing that face. She would stay. I named her Zola, after Zola Budd. Zola (the cat) and I were together for twenty-one and a half beautiful years.

Sitting at breakfast that Saturday morning in 2008, amid my friends' animated Olympics talk, my mind drifted back to Zola, and I realized that it had been almost four years since she left this earth. As I drove down Laguna Canyon Road, heading toward our farmer's market, I thought, *Maybe it's time to think about getting another cat.* I made a mental note to visit the Laguna Beach shelter. At that *very* moment, the loud ring of my cell phone jarred me out of my thoughts.

My longtime friend Kim's voice was practically shouting: "Miche! Where are you?!"

"On Laguna Canyon, heading to the farmer's market," I replied.

She ordered me to "Get here right away. Dick is holding a parking space for you—just get here quickly!"

Sure enough, there was Dick risking life and limb pushing other cars away and steering me into the space like a good concierge.

Kim pulled me by the arm to the market, to a man holding a small cage. Inside the cage was a small, very pissed-off, black and white "tuxedo," boy kitten. He explained that his son was highly allergic and they couldn't keep the kittens. I asked, "Kitten*s*?" Plural? Turns out there was a sister kitten back at the house. If he didn't find homes for them that day, they were going to the animal shelter.

Next thing I knew, we were in his jeep, driving to his home a quarter mile away. There at his house, was a little calico girl kitten racing all around their enclosed backyard. He told the story that a neighbor's cat had kittens. His children each picked one, and they named them Mollie and Oliver. He begged me to take them. And as Zola materialized by magic on my doorstep twenty-four years earlier, Mollie and Oliver arrived at my doorstep that afternoon, and a new journey began.

It only struck me hours later about the coincidence of the sequence of thoughts about Zola and going to the shelter along with Kim's urgent phone call. Those all led to Mollie and Oliver becoming an important part of my life, and I've felt grateful every day for those magical connections that brought us together.

Mollie Comes Home from the Hospital— "It's Simple"

Finally, the day arrived to bring Mollie home from the hospital. The doctor gave strict instructions to limit contact with Mollie to "one hour per day" over the next twelve days to minimize my radiation exposure. Apparently, cats can withstand a lot of radiation because they aren't exposed to it on a regular basis as people are. I asked if driving with her in the car counted against my one hour. He answered yes.

That was the "easy" part of this process. The doctor also proclaimed that Mollie showed some signs of kidney disease, necessitating giving her hydration injections every other day for twenty days. Egad! A skilled technician stepped in for my flash course in Injecting Reluctant Cats 101." She went very fast, saying it was *simple*, just hooking the bag on a rolling metal rack (which didn't go home with me. I had to find my own place to hang the bag), situating Mollie ("no sweat"), removing the cap off the needle, and putting the needle onto the syringe without stabbing myself, and finally the injection. Mollie was not amused.

They sent us home with a bag of liquid, one replacement bag, needles, and further cautionary instructions. Mollie cried the whole drive. My thoughts were elsewhere, pondering twelve days of trying to limit a cuddly-natured cat to one measly hour of contact each day.

And now, the idea of plunging a needle into my sweet cat was as far outside my comfort zone as it gets. *But*, I reminded myself, *this is what's needed to heal her*. So I repeated the mantra, "I can do hard things."

Upon arriving home, Mollie excitedly ran around the house,

ran to her brother Oliver and back to me. Oliver didn't seem to trust the medicinal smell, and I already had forty minutes of her radiation exposure, so I was doing my best to steer clear of her. However, Mollie kept rubbing against my leg or trying to get into my lap. I finally had to put her into the guest bedroom. I peeked in from time to time but had to shut the door quickly. Wow, that hurt—her as well as me. We all finally went to bed, having made it through our first day of radiation watch.

Friday, we got a fresh start. I tried to allocate more frequent, but shorter bursts of time with Mollie. It became much more challenging than anticipated to constantly be on watch duty with Mollie rubbing against my legs or jumping into my lap, and when the litterboxes needed to be emptied. Mollie is the cuddle bug in the family (although Oliver is a closet cuddle bug who plays it cool in public). Mollie is used to having full access to my lap, even during mediations. She looked so dejected whenever I pushed her away. I didn't want to keep her locked up all day, but soon realized it was not sustainable to allow her out daily for two weeks.

The next day was our first solo injection. Feelings of fear and discomfort flooded in, despite taking notes during the injection tutorial at the vet hospital. Using a hanger to hang the bag of liquid on the closet door eave, I removed the cap from the needle (took a few tries). Next, I needed to capture Mollie (by now suspicious of my intention). Not having the space of a veterinary office, the bathroom countertop became our injection site.

Mollie kept trying to escape, so I unscrewed the base of her cat carrier, laid a big towel inside, and put Mollie on the towel. She then needed to be positioned correctly to allow me to inject with my dominant, right hand. She immediately turned herself around. I turned her back around to the other side, and she reversed herself immediately. I realized the challenge in doing this by myself.

After several more attempts, she mustered up more strength

than I knew she had. Michelle: 0. Mollie: 1. With much awkwardness, my left elbow around and leaning over her, I grabbed her skin, and (with much praying) got the needle in. I had to simultaneously watch the bag, cat, and needle. By minute two, Mollie was trying to escape.

The moment the needle was removed, Mollie ran off. Phew! After giving Mollie her reward treats (as if her escape attempt deserved rewards), Mollie went back to her happy space. Counting up our time together, it was at least two hours of contact. I was exhausted, so I put Mollie to bed. She began her incessant cries. I laid down on my bed and cried. Oliver curled up next to me, and I fell asleep.

I awoke, mid-dream, approximately 4:00 a.m. Trying to open my eyes, I heard the familiar "purr" of . . . *Hmm, is that two cats?* I was jarred awake to see both cats, with their heads right next to mine on my pillow! OMG! I screamed and jumped off the bed. Both cats flew off the bed. My heart was racing! How long were they there? How much radiation did I get? And . . . into my brain! How on Earth did she get out of the guest room? Suspect number one was her brother Oliver. He's wily and crafty at getting doors opened. Based upon circumstantial evidence and past history, I adjudged Oliver guilty of busting Mollie out of jail.

The next injection was more difficult. Mollie pulled away, yanking the needle out. Liquid sprayed all around the bathroom until I caught the hose and needle and got everything back into order. Another time I stabbed myself with the needle, each injection a new adventure. But what truly broke my heart was each time, Mollie turned her head around, her eyes penetratingly staring into mine, telepathically saying, "How can you do this to me?!" My heart hurt for her, but it was important to keep my cat healthy and alive. Plus, we were almost done! So I kept moving forward saying the mantra: "We do hard things!"

Sometimes We Aren't in Control: Get over it! Surrender!

We finished the twelve days of limited contact, then counted down the days until the last injection, day twenty! Hooray!

One lesson learned: Clearly, a layperson giving a cat an injection, holding and keeping the cat still for three minutes of hydration delivery, is a *two*-person job. But the most important thing is, we were finished! Or so I thought.

We set up Mollie's checkup appointment and added Oliver who was a "tad" overweight and overdue for his checkup. I was serenaded during our drive by the cacophony from both cats howling in unison. I felt certain that other drivers could hear and were eyeing me suspiciously for cat torture. Meanwhile, I was in a good mood with high hopes for Mollie's recovery and Oliver having good health as well. I got part of my wish.

Hyperthyroidism in cats is fairly common. It can incapacitate and shorten the life of a feline. Upon diagnosing Mollie's condition, our veterinarian recommended two options. The first was pharmaceutical pills, which could abate the symptoms for a limited time. I tried the pill method first, and Mollie did well for several months. Then the medication became ineffective. I researched the radioiodine procedure, finally giving in to it as the best option.

You're probably wondering, *What does this treatment cost?* It's very expensive. The day I dropped Mollie off for her procedure, and during the lonely drive home, I thought about my blessings and gratitude to be able to afford a treatment such as this. Then another thought crept in, making me shudder. There are hundreds, likely thousands of avid animal lovers in this world who would do anything to save their pets. Sadly, many lack financial resources to do so. The mere thought of not being able to give our pets a chance at survival, when like here, there is a 95% chance of success, brought tears to my eyes. I've heard from too many friends who had their pets put down because treatment cost too much. I couldn't stop thinking that something had to be done to fix that.

Today was judgment day to find out if the procedure cured Mollie's hyperthyroidism. The 95% cure rate was comforting. I expected only good news.

Mollie's vet came in and said she had good and bad news. Uh oh! The good news was Mollie was cured from the hyperthyroidism. That was great! However, once that was removed, it revealed another condition: advanced kidney disease. I asked what that all meant; she said Mollie was at level 3.5 out of a total of 4, which is terminal; she was nearly there! I couldn't believe what I heard!

She said Mollie would have to go on special kidney food, and I needed to continue the injections. I burst into tears and blurted out, sounding childish, "I can't do it! I can't do that to my cat any longer! I thought we were done with them." She was grave in talking about the seriousness of her kidney condition.

I had been a tough, strong trial lawyer, transitioned to mediator, and thought I could handle and get through just about anything. My job in both careers has been to find solutions, solve problems. However, Mollie's new medical condition and treatment elevated my emotions, filling me with fear and insecurity. Further unsettling was the discovery that I was *not* in control.

Our vet suggested hiring a technician to help, which I did. I negotiated the weekly injections down to twice a week.

Poor Mollie wasn't the only one suffering. Oliver had issues, as the doctor declared him morbidly overweight with arthritis. As kittens, they were big with big paws, so their size seemed normal. Oliver needed to go on glucose diet food. We all went on a diet together.

Deja Vu with Round Two Injections

The first day of round two of injections arrived. I tried to sneak the technician inside, but cats have strong intuitions, and Mollie hid under the bed. It took both of us lying on the floor, cajoling, to no avail, finally using a broom to get her out from below, and the technician caught her. She gave the injection, but Mollie was miserable and fought us every step. Each session went like that, until neither of us could capture Mollie. She hissed, bared her teeth, and clawed at both of us. If we caught her at all, she was highly stressed and acted as if tortured, trying to escape.

Finally, neither the technician, nor our combined efforts would help us capture Mollie and drag her out for her injection. I finally decided Mollie knows best about her body. In resignation, I thanked the technician and called the vet. I said, "Neither she nor I can do this anymore." I could see Mollie's pain through her eyes. She communicated to me, *I've got this, let me be.* I was torn between my fabulous vet who I trust, and Mollie's sad, mistrustful face, plus my intuition and gut feeling. I finally said, "We are done with injections!" Afterward, I wondered if I was helping Mollie, or expediting the end of her life.

Animal Reiki to the Rescue!

Not knowing what to expect from there, Mollie continued to eat her kidney food, and I prayed for the best. Then two promising signs showed up. First, on a Saturday, at our local farmer's market, the ayurvedic health stand where I buy anti-inflammatory and other health products displayed a kidney healing treatment. I lamented, "I wish there was a kidney product for cats." The owner said, "This is suitable for cats! Just give a pinch instead of a teaspoon." I bought some and started putting a pinch of it in Mollie's food.

The second was more of an epiphany. I began a journey of Reiki training by Reiki Master Jacquie Freeman, who I met in a Jack Canfield Program. She offered giving Reiki to program members. Having received Reiki years earlier in Peru, I readily accepted the offer, and it was a wonderful experience. Reiki is a holistic healing modality using energy transfer from all around us. Generally done without touching, there are many pieces to what Reiki is. After a year of going through Jacquie's training workshops, I became a Level 3 Reiki Master. In my early training, I asked Jacquie if Reiki could be used to heal a cat's kidney disease? She said yes! I studied animal Reiki, and so began Mollie's Reiki sessions. Oliver displayed an interest too (as long as it didn't impede breakfast).

It was now a full year after we began this journey, and time for Mollie's and Oliver's checkup appointments. I was looking forward to finding out the kidney stats. I've done all the prayers, visualizations, ayurvedic tonics, and Reiki treatments, picturing the veterinary doctor looking with surprise at Mollie and declaring, "She's healed!" But . . . reminding myself that I'm not in control, I allowed myself to surrender. It was now in God's and the Universe's hands.

The doctor did her exam and said Mollie looked good. The following Tuesday, test results showed Mollie's kidney stats had *decreased*! She went down from 3.5, near terminal, to level 2! Her instructions were "Keep doing what you've been doing!"

To cap our good news, Oliver lost over two pounds (which for a cat is a lot) and was out of the danger zone as well.

Contemplation and Taking Back (Some) Control

With the proclamation that what we were doing for Mollie seemed to be working, I could finally sit and process this journey we had been on. Several things came to mind.

First, the veterinary treatments for Mollie were not inexpensive. My gratitude journal often included being able to afford my cat's medical care. The radiation-iodine treatment cost in the thousands. Even their recent wellness checks with the blood work cost over $700 total for both of them.

My sister Laurie has been an avid pet and animal advocate for decades. She was immersed in the passionate movement by animal lovers to create better conditions at animal shelters to find foster and adoptive parents for unwanted dogs and cats and other creatures. I tried to help when I could and finally offered to be a financial resource when animals needed medical care. My other sister, Beth, upon retiring, took on the arduous task of helping to rescue horses who were at auction or otherwise destined for death. She has become somewhat of a horse whisperer in helping to rehabilitate and train horses.

Some of the shelters can only be described as squalid and dismal. I am very grateful to the many no-kill shelters such as the one we have in Laguna Beach.

Which next brings up the magical coincidences through which Mollie and Oliver were delivered to me. I have often thought we get guided to do things we have no intention or prior thought of doing. It's fascinating to think of all that had to happen to bring these events to reality, as if the Universe was planning the way through which Mollie and Oliver would find a home. I even wondered if these special kittens were already destined to need medical care down the road, and fortunately, as a lawyer and mediator, I would be able to withstand the rigors and cost of that care. Perhaps my imagination is going too far. However it happened, I am quite certain that our being united was no accident.

It was further magical how one Reiki treatment in Peru led to meeting Jacquie, a very experienced multi-attuned Reiki Master and retired teacher. Thus, I had the good fortune to be trained by Jacquie as my Reiki guide. That Reiki training, in turn, undoubtedly helped with Mollie's healing and calming Oliver. It has also had a positive role in my own life.

I have always believed that things happen for reasons, although sometimes we can't imagine what that reason is at the time. It usually shows itself, even if it takes a while. I imagine some people will perceive these comments as woo-woo thinking; however, I have always been analytical. My college major at UCI (University of California, Irvine) was math, and I went on to law school, both studies built on analytical thinking.

Several lessons came from my experience with Mollie and Oliver, which I'm sharing in the hope that someone else may benefit.

1. We can do hard things. We *are* capable of being and doing more than the limits we set in our mind.

Think of your own life and times you were forced to move through your fear. We've all done it but likely don't dwell on that painful situation. It's worthy of remembrance to inspire us the next time we are faced with a dilemma that we've made it through before, and we have the resilience and will to get us through again.

2. We are always receiving messages, sometimes quiet and subtle, almost whispers, but we too often ignore them. I learned that all messages should be listened to, as long as they are evaluated for their good or bad aspects. If we don't listen to the quiet messages, guess what? We'll get *louder* messages! I've learned the hard way, as I have been on a quest toward gaining balance in my life. However, I ignored two auto-immunes and a concussion. Don't do what I did. I mean this in all seriousness: Listen to your *gut*. It is a direct connector to the *brain*. If you think something isn't right, it may not be. With medical care, with the utmost love and respect for each and every medical practitioner in my or my pets' lives, if you feel there is another path, don't dismiss it. Instead, sit in stillness, ponder, research other options if that is what you are feeling.

3. I hope to empower you to have the confidence in your decisions and get comfortable being "out of control." Sometimes the best thing we can do is surrender and have faith in those decisions.

4. Finally, when our heart is telling us something should be different, think about what you can do about it. We all have the ability to do something, even small, to help others.

Like many people, I have pondered "Why am I here?" and "What is my purpose?" In thinking about the chain of events, it seemed clear that these "magical" events go beyond mere coincidences.

Through this journey, and all of the epiphanies that planted themselves before me, I see my path to a purpose. I feel so grateful and blessed to be able to provide the needed level of care for my pets and feel an urgency to create as my legacy (and yours), a foundation to assist other cat parents in caring for their sick cats. This is why I feel so passionately about creating this foundation and funding to address skyrocketing medical expenses, the lack of home visits, and further education about ways to provide care to our pets. My hope is to set up a foundation that will help support pet parents and pets facing these challenging decisions; that will provide help to those who cannot afford medical care for their pets, thereby giving them the power and potential for saving their pets, instead of going the route of euthanasia.

I encourage you to be open hearted and receptive, and brace yourself when stepping into your own legacy. My wish is to inspire you and others to not always go with the flow of the usual, to be able to listen to your gut and intuition regardless of how unusual, unique, and outrageous something may seem—to hear it, not just dismiss it. Wishing you all good health and guardian angels overseeing your fur babies.

ABOUT MICHELLE A. REINGLASS

Who am I? Here's the short answer: I'm Michelle Reinglass, reformed lawyer turned mediator, international speaker and best-selling author, Reiki Master, and balance expert . . . a.k.a. animal lover.

In other words, I'm a poly-hyphenate.

Here's what I really do:

(1) As a mediator, I help people negotiate through the tunnel of conflict, emotions, betrayal, mistrust, hurt, pain, and anger to seeing the bright light of day and their path to peace.

(2) As a Reiki Master, I help restore, realign, and re-energize their body, mind, and spirit.

(3) As a balance mentor, I teach people how to live their life in flow, learn to focus on what is important and say no to what's not, to feel more in control of their time and set appropriate boundaries, which leads to discovering and achieving their perfect "imperfect" level of balance.

In the end, my goal is to help empower people to reach their state of flow and balance, protect and defend themselves from toxic conflict, overwhelm, and burnout. And encourage them to live the life they dream of designing.

OUR DEEPEST TRUTHS

Lisa Marie Runfola

It was otherwise indistinguishable from any other morning in the fall of 2020. We were midway through the pandemic and fully set in our routines as a family by that point. Both of our youngest girls were upstairs on Zoom. Andrew, as far as I knew, was in the master suite preparing for his day. I was in my office when I got a call from Enzo.

"Mama, Andrew won't answer the phone."

On the one hand, this is the type of mundane activity I've tried to extract myself from with my older kids. Enzo was in college. His ability or inability to get through to his stepfather wasn't my business. And anyway, it probably wasn't an emergency.

On the other hand, something in me perked up. Andrew was *never* without his phone—ideally, he had both his personal and his work phones on him at all times, and even if he were in a meeting, he would surely text Enzo and let him know when he would return the call. It was the two-year anniversary of Andrew's mother's death, and I wondered if he was having a hard time with that. In any case, something just didn't feel right, so, while still on the phone with my son, I went down the hall in search of my husband.

The bathroom door was closed, so I knocked. Andrew's initial answer was a weak, almost animal sound; when he regained his words, he indicated that he was having stomach trouble and would be a few minutes. I'm horrified to say that at this moment, Enzo and I joked around a little bit about Andrew's illness. You know, nothing mean, just standard bathroom humor. But Andrew wasn't laughing on the other side of the door. I thought again about it being the anniversary of his mother's death and backed off.

I knocked again a minute or two later and asked if he could open the door so I could at least see him. Shortly thereafter, I heard the toilet and the sink, then the lock clicking in the door. A man who looked something like my husband and something like what the cat dragged in emerged.

He sat down on the edge of the bed and held his head in his hands. "Wow, it's really bad. It hit me out of nowhere. I feel just awful."

"You look pretty bad," I said, perhaps unhelpfully. I told Enzo I would call him back and hung up the phone. As I moved to sit beside Andrew, he laid back, reclining on the bed. His skin had taken on a tone I had never seen before—he was almost gray, and there were beads of sweat forming on his forehead.

I was sure it was COVID. With a high-risk child in the house, we had all been careful to not contract it, but there was remodeling going on in our home, and some contact with others was simply unavoidable. And sure, diarrhea and poor coloring weren't necessarily COVID symptoms, but this had come on quickly, as if out of nowhere. In my mind, I was imagining how I was going to quarantine him from the rest of us.

As I went to prepare a cold washcloth, I peppered him with questions: how close did he stand to the contractor the other day, had he been careful to mask when he had gone out the day before? But as I returned to the bedroom and saw him, I knew that COVID or not, we were in over our heads. Somehow, in the thirty seconds I had been gone, he had become even grayer.

When I said the word *hospital*, my normally tough-as-nails husband didn't even argue. He agreed, then went upstairs to let the girls know we were leaving. Later, he'd tell me that he had knocked on both of our daughters' doors and said goodbye because he had a strange feeling it might be the last time he would see them.

We got to the hospital within minutes. It's right across the street from our house, but I drove him because he didn't look well enough to walk. The staff wouldn't let me into the ER due to pandemic restrictions. I watched through the glass as a staffer signaled that they would first get him checked in and then give me a call. I wandered reluctantly back to my car and drove back across the street.

The next hour was a bit of a blur. I went back to my desk and tried to work, vaguely unsettled that Andrew was in the hospital but not overly worried. Then, the phone rang.

The nurse first asked questions to determine that it was me on the other end of the line, which I answered slightly impatiently. "Yes, it's me, Lisa Marie Runfola; yes, Andrew is my husband; yes, the tall one, pretty good-looking when he isn't completely gray and dehydrated; yes, yes, yes."

"Okay, Lisa Marie, I'm so glad to have you on the phone. So I'm calling from cardiology, and your husband will be admitted for surgery shortly."

Wait—what?

I tried to argue with her; in the rush at the hospital, they must have switched his chart with some *other* tall, gray-skinned Andrew, because my husband had diarrhea, or maybe COVID. I explained that he had just had an EKG as part of a check-up some months before and everything was fine. She clearly refuted what I had to say, explaining that despite his earlier EKG, my husband, *my Andrew*, had 100% blockage in the front of his heart and was being prepped for emergency surgery, and that we had gotten him to the hospital just in the nick of time.

Within one or two minutes, she explained that they would call when they knew more and hung up. My eyes flickered toward the window, where across the street, my husband was going into emergency surgery and fighting for his life. I put my elbows up on the desk and held my head in my hands. I closed my eyes and tried to breathe.

When I opened my eyes, I saw my calendar blotter on the desk in front of me. It's really the whole family's calendar blotter, and it's filled with appointments in different ink, with days that spill over their allotted box and appointments that have been crossed out and rescheduled multiple times. I looked at the busy week ahead, and the one after that. *How are we going to do all that while Andrew is having a heart attack?* I wondered.

In my panic, I decided that the best thing I could do was clear the calendar for the whole family for the next two weeks. I started firing off emails and making things happen. Yet in the back of my mind, I was desperately trying to understand what was happening.

I must have asked myself four hundred questions in about two minutes. *Is this real? How could this have happened? How did I miss the signs?* Eventually, the questions began to coalesce into the main question I find myself asking whenever I'm surprised or shocked by life's events—the question that has become my guiding light in my work as an author, podcaster, speaker, and life coach:

What's not being said here?

* * *

Over the last few years, I've developed a sort of affinity for deriving what's not being said—or at least sniffing out the presence of an unsaid thing, even if I don't know exactly what it is. When conversation and connection take place on the surface level, it *bothers* me. It just feels wrong. Seen from that angle, my sixth sense for what's not being said is part superpower, part allergy.

Looking back, I can see that I was always a bit intuitive, and I was always bothered by the presence of what's not being said. I've always noticed when there's an unspoken truth waiting to be aired. This tendency became a full-blown habit when I put some of my own hardest truths out in the open and published my memoir, *A Limitless Life in a Powerless World*. That book was years in the making, and by the time it was published in 2019, I was ready to say it all—so I did.

The experience of putting my deepest inner experience out into the public changed me. It forever shifted my relationship with shame and fear because I learned once again that telling the absolute truest truth I know makes me the strongest version of myself. In the wake of my memoir's publication, as I connected with readers from all over the world who were drawn in by my story, I developed an even stronger intuitive ability to detect *anything* short of the full emotional truth in myself and others.

I understand that I may be an uncommon type; a lot of people would rather just talk on the surface. Yet I no longer have time or energy for that. It's just not for me. I've made my pros and cons lists, and I now know that saying what's not being said is non-negotiable when it relates to me and my life. I won't push anyone else to join me on this—participation in my no-holds-barred, saying-the-hardest-thing reality is entirely voluntary—but I know what's right for me.

I've gone through the absolute worst-case scenario of holding something that's not being said, and it brought me as close to soul death as I've ever come. I was nearly lifeless; I had no joy, no connection to my higher purpose. When I think back to those times, my throat immediately tightens and my stomach begins to hurt. These are precisely the same sensations I experience when I'm talking to someone and I sense there's something that isn't being said. These sensations irritate me, nagging at me, begging me to *say something* until I think I might go absolutely crazy.

The truth is that there are plenty of reasons to not say things—and some things really are better left unsaid. Saying the unsaid thing can cause our whole life to explode. It can hurt a relationship and cost money and cause tears. If done prematurely, saying the thing that's not being said can cause more pain than relief. Many people may recognize and evaluate what's not being said but still choose not to say it, and I understand that choice.

Yet often there are really important reasons to say what's not being said. Speaking a truth aloud is what facilitates change; it isn't a guarantee that something will change, but it's the only way it's possible. For instance, one of my coaching clients experienced a massive personal breakthrough when she was finally able to admit to herself that she had a troubled relationship with her mother and had created a maternal bond with her grandmother as a result. She felt a sense of relief that simply would not have been possible had she not been able to give space to the grief she felt about her relationship with her mother.

Often, just stating a need aloud gets it met, either because another person or a higher power hears the request and responds. Another of my coaching clients, a mother herself, shared how her young adolescent daughter started having emotional breakdowns about a year into the pandemic. These emotional events started manifesting in physical illness that only resolved when the daughter was able to express her need for more "fun" time with her mother in the absence of peers—which, of course, her mother was immediately happy to provide.

These two examples show that as scary as it is, saying what's not being said can have a swift and undeniable effect. They prevent a buildup of emotion that can be hard to break down, and that can lead to disastrous consequences.

* * *

The surgeon called me and I answered on the first ring. Though the surgery had been a success, it had ended up being more complicated than expected. The surgeon explained that it was extremely common for men Andrew's age to have these sudden, catastrophic cardiac events. Even seemingly healthy men who had just had an EKG. Even men who never clutched their arm or felt chest pain, but instead just had gray skin and stomach symptoms.

Andrew had what is called a widowmaker, a complete arterial blockage. He would go on to have another surgery several days later. While he spent over a week in the cardiac unit across the street, he wasn't able to receive a single visitor.

Andrew went through this ordeal on one side of the street while our family experienced our own whirlwind set of emotions on the other. On multiple occasions, he came close to death. In a situation like that, I've learned that the only thing anyone can really do is put one foot in front of the other and try to make it through—and luckily, Andrew and our family got through it. But it wasn't easy.

I worked to manage the household on my own and keep showing up for the kids, each of whom had their own individual needs. At some point, I realized that I'd had to somewhat *become* Andrew to keep the family going. Andrew has always been the strong one, the one that others turned to when they needed help. Whether the help was financial or logistical or anything else, Andrew would usually step up to do it himself, or in rare circumstances he would enlist someone else to get the job done. This was true in our family unit but also in his family of origin. Andrew is a Scorpio; he's stubborn, and he doesn't quit.

The anniversary of his mother's death brought a good deal of unspoken grief to the surface. Andrew and his mother were very close, and she brought out a certain side in him. Around her, he would finally stop working and relax a little bit, enjoying the small pleasures of life. Though he had been grieving her for two years and managing her estate as well, he hadn't taken a vacation or stopped working; he hadn't had much time to deal with the feelings surrounding her death at all. Meanwhile, the world hadn't given him much of a break in return; though we all still relied on him, his heart simply had nothing else to give. For the first time, our heroic rescuer needed to be rescued.

Later, Andrew would tell me what this time was like for him. He had a lot of time to think about it, after all. He explained that he was carrying baggage willingly, not knowing the damage it was doing to him. He realized that there were things for him to face and address regarding the grief he felt for his mother in order to move on. The heart attack did what he couldn't: demand the space and time needed to process it all.

As my husband struggled for his life in the hospital, I began questioning what I could have said to him that might have mitigated his heart attack. I could have taken more off his plate, let him know I was here for him more, helped him open up more. It wasn't just about what he wasn't saying—it was about what I wasn't saying too.

I realized that while I could make it complicated and detailed, there was also a very simple way to describe what Andrew wasn't saying: "Help." And there was a very simple way to describe what I wasn't saying too: "How can I help you?"

* * *

When Andrew had his heart attack, my coaching practice was just taking off. I had officially launched myself as a life coach and was seeing clients. The heart attack presented me with a clear opportunity to understand how what's not being said can build up and manifest in our lives, like the way uncleared dryer lint builds slowly, slowly, until it starts a fire. I found myself wanting to share this with my clients.

I was able to do so with some of them. With others, I noticed they put up a wall, so I made space for it, because saying what's not being said is largely dependent on timing; each one of us has our moment. My goal as a coach is simply to support each client as they reach their own moment, then hold space for them when they speak.

Sometimes it helps to know that saying what's not being said doesn't mean you need to act on it—at least, not right now. It doesn't require you to do anything or change anything, especially if you're only saying it to yourself or to someone neutral that you trust, like a friend or coach. For some people, years can go by between when they admit to themselves what is truly happening and when they act on it, and as long as they're not being hurt by it, I consider it a natural part of the process.

It's important to understand that this isn't a one-time fix. We don't just get to say it all once and then consider it done. It's an ongoing process of uncovering and revealing our truths, first to ourselves, then to those we trust, and then to the world. I'm still in this process, as are my coaching clients and everyone else I know.

This is part of why working with a life coach can be so helpful. By installing a neutral, supportive person in our lives who can hold space for all our deepest, most unsayable truths, we support a process that's happening anyway, whether we like it or not. Darkness is always moving toward light—that's part of the human experience. A good life coach isn't going to push you before you're ready, but if your secret is what is causing your darkness, she will turn on the light. Out of love and compassion, a good life coach can shine the light on your deepest, darkest parts.

* * *

Andrew is still in his recovery process, but modern medicine has treated him well, and the doctors assure us he has every chance of living for decades to come. As a family, we're all working to take more off his plate—giving greater responsibility to the kids who are now adults and teens and making time for vacations and breaks. I've worked to teach the kids that, whenever possible, they can call me first with a problem. And I've become downright insistent about making him delegate family tasks. I no longer ask what I can do; instead, every day I ask him, "What is the one thing I can take off your plate right now?"

I've had to become just as insistent about our new vacation plan—but so far, I've been successful. We bought a home on Nantucket where we can spend intentional time as a family, just as we used to spend time at his mother's villa. We're learning to honor what she brought to the family by recreating at least part of it for Andrew.

I continue to coach clients on what's not being said as well as promote the idea of speaking our deepest truths through my podcast. I also continue to work on searching for what's not being said in me, because once again, this simply isn't a one-time fix; it's an ongoing process. In the sixteen months since Andrew's heart attack, we've grown as people, as a couple, and as a family.

In a few weeks, we're going to Nantucket, and Andrew is taking three weeks—yes, that's twenty-one days—off from work. No work phone. No internet. No projects. Only toes-in-the-sand fun! We almost always enjoy our time together as a family. Still, knowing we nearly lost our chance to have moments like this makes them all the sweeter.

ABOUT LISA MARIE RUNFOLA

Lisa Marie Runfola is an author, speaker, certified Levin Life Coach, and the host of the podcast *What's Not Being Said.* She brings her honest, imperfect, and joyful life into her writing and speaking, and her coaching leads other adventurous souls through the process of speaking their deepest truths and getting unstuck. As a mother of five, Lisa Marie lives a limitless life while actively parenting her two youngest at home. Her work is engaging and remarkably funny, encouraging others to break free of what holds them back and live the life that has been waiting for them all along. Lisa Marie's first book, *A Limitless Life in a Powerless World: A Memoir,* was released in 2019, and she is hard at work on her second book, *Unstuck: An Adventurous Soul's Guide to Feeling Stuck, Getting Free, and Everything In Between.* She and her family currently split their time between their homes in Lake Forest, Illinois; Sarasota, Florida; Nantucket, Massachusetts; and Ascona, Switzerland. You can find her on Instagram at @lisamarierunfola, check out her author page on Facebook, see what she's thinking at @authorlmrunfola on Twitter, or find *What's Not Being Said* wherever you get your podcasts.

To work with Lisa Marie directly, check out
www.lisamarierunfola.com

PUTTING THE PIECES BACK TOGETHER

Samantha Ruth

I don't know how I did 2019. Any of it. All of it. When I look back at it now, when I look back at *me*, I see such a shell of the person I am.

And at the time, I thought I had come so far. And I had!

Should I back up? A lot of you know my story, but even more of you don't. I'm Sam, the tomboy, the sports fan, daddy's little girl, the music-loving hippie, the vegetarian, the outdoorsy, nature-loving, star-gazing, convertible-driving Sam.

I'm a psychologist. I'm a fur mommy. I'm an aunt. A sister. A daughter.

I'm a Scorpio. Sensitive. Passionate. Organized (OCD anyone?) A recovering perfectionist. A woman with anxiety—since before I can remember.

A widow.

I'm originally from Michigan, and I moved to Colorado in 2014 to marry Jim, the one and only love of my life, the one who got away, my best friend, my soulmate. My everything.

Sassy (my pit bull mix who was one and a half at the time and is now ten) and I left our friends, family, my thriving psychology practice, and the only life I'd ever known to start our new life with Jim in Denver.

I wish I could say *the end*. Because my life was literally my fairy tale. Until it wasn't. But I'm skipping things again.

I'm the girl who never struggled in school. The girl who never struggled professionally. Work, performing, achieving—these things come naturally to me.

Even when I convinced myself I wouldn't get into Michigan . . . when I started over professionally (after Jim and I broke up in our twenties) in Livonia, Michigan, a completely unfamiliar area to me at the time . . . success happened quickly. Correction: I created success quickly.

And while I moved to Denver solely for my life with Jim, I also had my lifelong dreams of changing the way the world views mental health. So I started doing what I do. I immediately found an office. The mountain views . . . beyond breathtaking.

And off I went. Going into schools. Introducing myself. Reaching out to the courts. I won't get started on the differences in mental health care from Michigan to Colorado.

Or the licensing roller coaster rides. Or the fact that absolutely everything is dictated by the government here. But it's true, and it's not just isolated to my field.

Back to me. Plain and simple? I got rejected. Not once. Every single time. I worried that I was disappointing Jim, who only cared about my happiness, not my success. I absolutely was disappointing myself. And losing confidence. And gaining anxiety. Rapidly.

It wasn't about success or income, let me be clear. It was about doing what I love. Because I've always said—and meant—that it's not what I do. It's who I am. And that piece was missing in Colorado.

But I had Jim. We had our life. I fell in love with Colorado. And even when I was bedridden before back surgery, I still was the luckiest girl in the world.

I knew what life was like without Jim from our time apart. And I cherished every single moment—we both did. The nurses said I was the happiest person post-surgery they had ever seen.

We immediately started planning things again. I had many months of recovering ahead of me, but the pain that had been with me for so long was finally gone, and I felt like me again.

Road trips. Concerts. Hikes. It was all in the planner.

And then, on an ordinary Wednesday, my phone wouldn't stop ringing. It was Jim's office. He collapsed at the microwave waiting for his lunch, and paramedics were taking him to the hospital.

So much of this is a blur, but an hour later my life was over. December 27, 2017. The day I became a widow, a word that took me well over a year to even say. The day my world shattered into millions of pieces.

I don't have the words to explain the level of pain and anxiety 2018 was filled with for me.

I won't give you a rundown of the full year, but I'll share *the* pivotal moment:

The moment I didn't listen to others and what they thought was best for me. The moment I listened to *me*—possibly for only the second time in my life. The first was when I took that job in Livonia that absolutely catapulted my career.

My loved ones wanted me to accept a different offer, one with a more secure income. I can't even imagine what my life would look like without my time in Livonia. I definitely wouldn't have reconnected with Jim . . .

Back to 2018. This time, my loved ones didn't want me and Sassy to go to Grand Lake for my first wedding anniversary without Jim. They worried about me driving alone, being overcome with emotions.

And I understood all the concerns. But I literally felt like I *had* to go. Something bigger than me was calling me there.

So I didn't listen to them. And I had a week that absolutely changed my life.

I decided to get Sassy a sister, Dallas, who immediately brought joy back into our home and hearts—when joy is something I never believed I'd feel again.

I decided to take *another* (feedback from those others who want what's best for me again!) year off to train with Jack Canfield, a lifelong mentor of mine.

Until this point, I was surviving. Doing what was expected. Going through the motions. Now, for the first time, I wanted to do these things . . . for me. For me and Sassy. And Dallas! And always, for Jim.

Within two months of being part of the Canfield Family, I connected with Kate Butler: a piece of my journey that literally hasn't just changed my life, it saved my life. She saw me—correction, she sees me—in ways that I just don't see myself.

I write to Jim every day. I've always written. And while I was feeling lost and unproductive, Kate helped me see that others needed to hear my story. As much as I needed to share it to heal.

So hello, 2019. To the world, from the outside, 2019 looked like Sam traveling to Nashville, California, Chicago, Arizona. Trainings and retreats and certifications and personal growth.

I became a best-selling author for the first time. I was featured on the Times Square billboard.

But inside I was still drowning in pain. I was still lost professionally. Kate laughs every time I say this, but it's the truth: I didn't care about other people's problems.

I was literally just doing what felt right. Without knowing why. And without any sort of plan. At all!

That's not me. I'm the girl who lived by my planner. The girl who was always working on the next task, the next goal to achieve.

And here I was, doing what felt right. Without any idea

whatsoever what was next. I learned that the unknown is beautiful. I learned to trust the process. Trust the universe. Trust myself.

I started to see so many things I was missing as I cruised through life according to my planner.

Mind you, up until these moments, I was the girl who laughed at phrases like "trust the universe." Meditation "didn't work" for me, and I was too literal for any of the woo-woo.

And now, the woo-woo was my path. My power. I literally was letting go of lifelong pieces of me, replacing them with new, healthier pieces. The old ones didn't seem to fit anymore.

Another pivotal moment actually came during a meditation. I was supposed to open a box and find something inside . . . except all I could see was shattered pieces. Colorful shards.

Like the shattered pieces of my life when I lost Jim.

I started thinking about things like a logo when I didn't even know what my logo was for! I still didn't care about other people's problems.

But things were starting to happen. The connections I made throughout 2019 fueled me. I decided 2020 was going to be my year of "returning to life."

I went to a training in Canada and began really focusing on what was next for me professionally. My now partner Claudia and I created Faces of Mental Illness, our movement to change the way the world views mental illness.

My bigger picture was beginning to unfold. And I knew I had to get out of Denver. I absolutely hated it without Jim. (I didn't love it with him, let's be honest!) I should mention that I knew I wanted (and needed) to move months earlier, but I was getting distracted by my loved ones piping in again with what they thought was best.

So I decided to sell our house. An extremely emotional decision. I still hadn't gone through Jim's clothes. His office. But I knew it was time.

I got offers within two days of listing it. And then COVID happened.

I literally sold my house and wasn't allowed to go look for another one. I made the decision that it was time to start doing life again. And the world told me nope. Not yet, Sam!

It felt so impossible to find a house. Overwhelming. They sold before I even had time to look. And I just couldn't decide where exactly I wanted to live.

Something made me consider renting, which Jim wouldn't do financially, but I felt him pushing me to consider. We rented for two years before we bought our house. "I know where I want to live. Do you know where we want to live?" Jim would ask me.

And I didn't. And this felt the same . . . only with a deadline! And wouldn't ya know there was a house in Boulder . . . Boulder, where I would never have looked to buy because it was light-years out of my price range.

I always loved it there. It reminds me of Ann Arbor (go blue) and this, too, felt like a sign. I had been saying to everyone for months that I want to live in the middle of nowhere but five minutes away from everything.

And this house was way north in Boulder and exactly that. Okay, it was ten to fifteen minutes away from everything. But I loved it and moved only weeks later.

Packing and physically leaving *our* house is another experience I can't find the words to explain. Moving is stressful during the best of the times. The emotions, the pain, were both so real. So raw. But I knew it was the next missing piece.

I felt the shift immediately. New energy. New surroundings. New everything. And others *saw* the shift. Almost instantly, people were saying things like "Something is different."

And it was. I was.

Even in the middle of COVID. In a new, unfamiliar area. Things started happening.

I said to a friend that I needed rehab for grief. Because there's rehab for everything else, and here I was, now two-plus years without Jim, and I still wasn't okay.

Remember everything I did in 2019? The world was seeing my external progress, but no one could see how exhausting each and every step was. Things that used to come easily to me suddenly overwhelmed me.

And I needed help. I wanted a personal helper, and I'm not kidding. Not for work. For life. And through that honesty, Griefhab was born.

I suddenly had more professional direction and motivation than I had in years. I knew the world of stigmas in mental health both as a psychologist and a lifelong anxiety sufferer. But now I was living in a world that also judges and stigmatizes grief.

My new mission was unfolding: to change the way the world views both mental illness *and* grief. I became extremely passionate about helping others understand that we have to heal our way, that the world doesn't know what's best for us!

That it takes tuning *out* that noise and tuning *in* to our own voice. That each path is unique and perfect in its own way yet judged by the world all the same. That in order to heal, we have to do it *our way*.

I vowed to create the services I couldn't find for myself . . . with my expertise and resources! I had a new client before I was even looking, and as much as I had resisted this path, I innately knew it was *my* path.

It takes someone who's been there. Someone who gets it. Add my education and experience to my new life experience, and the result is that I can help in a way others can't.

The Be Ruthless Show: Making Noise and Breaking Stigmas was born next. I stumbled my way through technology and nerves to create a platform.

I cried all day when it launched. Because all the things I had worked so hard for in Denver, all the things I had worked so hard for with Jim, were happening now. Without him physically by my side to share the moments.

I could feel his pride everywhere. I know he's watching and with me absolutely always. I talk to him always. I write to him daily. He's a part of any and every decision.

And honoring his name and making him proud gives my life daily purpose. Internally. The piece that's been missing since he took his last breath. An internal reason to go on.

So while the world was locked down, I was professionally finding my place. Not only in Colorado (finally) but also in the world.

Even though I didn't understand it at the time, I did need this time before throwing myself back in "the real world." I became fully connected to my body. To my intuition. To my voice.

Decisions that used to come with so much internal back-and-forth now came easily. So much pressure, pressure I've carried my entire life, was immediately lifted.

I'm still me. I'm still an overthinker. I'm still sensitive. But I'm completely aware that I know me best. And that I know the signs—even if I don't know what they mean in the moment.

I had major water damage in May of 2021. The ceiling literally collapsed. It was a disaster—physically, obviously, but also emotionally.

I had a trip to visit my family in Michigan scheduled . . . my family that I hadn't seen in well over a year. The internal what-do-I-do struggle began, and then I found a lump on Sassy.

A mast cell tumor. I knew in an instant that my trip was clearly going to have to wait. I trusted the signs. The universe was telling me to *stay home*.

Of course I was devastated that my trip was postponed. But I didn't go back and forth over what to do. I eliminated all that mental stress.

So when there was a fire—in the middle of winter, mind you—my ears perked up. My body literally felt off. I should add that in October of 2020, there was also a fire. It felt like it was in my backyard. I was on the very brink of the evacuation lines, in this new area in the middle of nowhere.

I was traumatized. I immediately went back on my anxiety medication. And it really impacted me. In many ways and for many months.

I should also add that in my year and a half living in Boulder, I started to feel *too* in the middle of nowhere. Running to grab something at the store was a trip.

So when there was this second fire, I truly panicked. I didn't feel safe. I felt like I was in the area most at risk. Everyone said they'd never seen anything like it before, and it was unusual, not to worry.

That didn't comfort me. At all. While most were looking at insurance policies in case of future fires, I started looking at areas I'd feel safer living.

My loved ones thought I was being impulsive. Overreacting. Being Sensitive Sam.

I felt like I did before that first trip to Grand Lake without Jim. Like I absolutely had to do it. Something bigger than myself was telling me to move. *Now.*

And so I did. I let everyone voice their opinions, and I did what I knew was best. I found my way to Fort Collins.

Everything about it here feels right. I found an amazing house (much better suited for my podcast and work environment, by the way), and I once again packed and made the move.

Two days later, there was a fire in my old backyard. Literally. Do you get what I mean when I say, Can you imagine if I had listened to everyone else?

I wouldn't have connected with the Canfield Community and, therefore, Kate Butler Books. I wouldn't have Dallas. And I would have lived through another fire. And, and, and.

Here I am now, happily adjusting to my new life in Fort

Collins. It's an entirely new beginning. I don't know anyone here. I'm starting over. In every single way.

And for the first time in Colorado, it really feels like home. And, like I'm learning always happens, things started happening. Immediately.

I was offered a TV show to expand The Ruthless message. Stay tuned for *Authentically Ruthless*! I was asked to speak at a school, the big piece that has been missing my entire time in Colorado; I've absolutely missed working with teens and the schools.

And it is all just happening. Correction: I am making it happen. And I'm also focusing on me personally, again.

The girls and I went back to Grand Lake a couple weeks ago. I was overwhelmed thinking about that trip in 2018, crying under a tree with Sassy. Feeling so broken. So lost.

We sat under that same tree, and this time, I could see how very far I've come. In so many ways. Of course I have further to go, but I need to stress that it's not what matters.

It's the progress that matters. It's going from having absolutely no hope at all to having complete confidence. It's about knowing that I can handle absolutely anything life hands me. Knowing that I'm strong. Knowing that I matter.

And I need anyone who is struggling to know that you matter too. You're making hundreds of amazing steps even when it feels like you're completely stuck. It's hard to see them along the way sometimes, but they're happening. And you will see them eventually.

Make sure to stop and look for them along the way . . . because they're there. Each and every day.

I never believed I'd smile, let alone laugh, again. I believed that all my dreams had been shattered and that I would never have more.

And I'm here to tell you, happily, that I was wrong.

You will get through it. You're not alone, and you don't have to go through it alone. Connecting with my tribe was my biggest step—during that year off that others discouraged.

And now I'm helping others pick up their pieces. And it's not just about putting them back together again. It's about recognizing that the new version is beautiful.

It feels broken at first. For a while. But I'd like to help you redefine that perspective. I'd like to help you see that your perceived differences or weaknesses are actually your biggest gifts.

You don't have to hide them. Suffering in silence adds to the pain. Healing is about doing it *your way*. Picking up the pieces in your timeframe. At your pace.

It's about making yourself a priority, possibly for the first time! It's about tuning out the noise and tuning into yourself.

It's about being true to you. Ruthlessly.

ABOUT SAMANTHA RUTH

Samantha is a psychologist, speaker, best-selling author, and host of *The Be Ruthless Show*, a podcast dedicated to making noise and breaking stigmas. She helps people around the world turn their pain into their power by guiding them to be their true selves, not who they think they need to be, by embracing their differences and recognizing that their perceived weaknesses are their biggest strengths, and by living life on their own terms.

Samantha's mission is to change the way the world views both grief and mental health so people can speak about whatever issues they have and get the help they not only need but deserve without fear of judgment, labels, and repercussions.

Samantha is the proud founder of Griefhab, a 24/7 community open to anyone who has experienced a loss. After losing her husband, Sam learned personally how little support is available and vowed to create these services for others.

In her free time, you can find Sam and her pups, Sassy and Dallas, on one of their outdoor adventures. They love living in Colorado and never miss an opportunity to explore their beautiful surroundings. Music fuels Sam's soul, family means everything to her, and honoring her late husband, Jim, and making him proud gives her life daily purpose.

samantharuth.com
sam@samantharuth.com

LIFE IS HAPPENING FOR YOU

Lindsay Smith, LCSW

Eradicating the victim mentality.
Choosing to believe that life is happening for you.
Always. In all ways.

The victim mentality sucks the joy out of life and the energy out of you! You were made for more, and you can have it. You can love your life—*all* of it—now!

The victim mentality is more pervasive that we realize. It has crept into every facet of society.

We typically think of victim mentality as believing life is happening *to* you. Blaming life's challenges on others or on circumstances. Feeling like we have no control and like bad things always happen to us.

But it doesn't have to be this extreme. Feeling discouraged after receiving negative comments on social media. Feeling overwhelmed at work because things aren't happening as fast as you'd like and your to-do list keeps growing. Feeling upset that you missed your daughter's soccer game because you got called away to an important meeting. Even feeling frustrated that you hit another red light. All of these are subtle examples of the victim mentality.

The victim mentality often occurs subconsciously. But it

leaves us feeling powerless, and the joy we want to experience feels elusive.

It doesn't have to be like this. You can learn to release the victim mentality and *choose to believe that life is happening* for *you. Always. In all ways.*

And when you choose this, you begin experiencing deep, authentic joy on a daily basis.

Your life will never be the same.

How does this work? Events that happen in life are neutral; they are not inherently good or bad. We assign our own meaning to each event and the meaning we assign determines how we feel about the event.

Let me explain with an extreme example. Imagine a young teen is walking home after school and a gang member kills him in a drive-by shooting. A police officer at the end of her shift gets called to the scene. The streets are closed, and commuters are stuck in traffic. Of course, the mother of the young teen feels devastated as her child has been murdered. But the gang member feels proud. The policer officer is feeling frustrated and sad because she won't be able to pick up her son from school for the special date they planned. And the commuters feel irritated because they are delayed. The event is the same, yet the meaning assigned by each person is very different. And how each person feels is determined by the meaning *they* assigned to the event.

The life-changing choice is to believe life is happening for *us in every situation.* Sometimes the reason why it's happening becomes clear, but many times it doesn't. The clarity around why or how life is happening for us is not the driving factor. We choose to believe this simply because it gives us a sense of power and hope and brings more joy into our life.

If each of the people in the example above believed life was happening for them, they might think or feel the following:

- The mother of the teen would still feel devastated, but when she is ready to free herself from the unbearable grief, she begins to move forward by embracing the belief that life is happening for her. She does this while holding her love for her son in her heart and allowing it to encourage and inspire her rather than keep her down. Choosing this belief doesn't mean she wanted her son to be murdered; it simply means she is choosing to believe and trust that life is happening *for* her, even when she can't see it clearly, because it allows her to feel better. It gives her hope and courage to move forward.

- The police officer who believes life is happening for her is glad that she can use her training to support this grieving mother and help find the murderer and is grateful her son gets to go to a movie with his best friend.

- The commuter who believes life is happening for them appreciates the time in the car to continue listening to their audio book, to plan out the meals for the next week, or to simply enjoy some unusual quiet time.

Choosing to believe that life is happening for us does not mean that sadness, pain, and other challenging emotions don't exist. It just gives us a way to free ourselves from staying stuck inside these emotions, and it empowers us to move forward and live a life full of joy and meaning.

We learn to listen to our own internal guidance and knowing. We open ourselves up to unlimited joy and abundance.

From this wellspring of joy, we experience resiliency and comfort and ease in our own skin, in who we are. We don't take events so personally. Instead, we choose to believe that each event happened for our benefit.

In a very uncertain world, we have incredible certainty in our own personal power as we choose to believe that everything that happens in our life is serving us in some way, whether we can readily identify it or not. This knowing creates a cascade of confidence, creativity, and connection.

We open ourselves up to deep, authentic joy—in each moment and in our life overall.

From this place of joy, we are also able to embrace profound self-love. Wholly loving ourselves not only feels amazing and creates unshakable confidence, but it also serves as a great example for those we love.

Choosing to believe life is happening for us elevates our relationships. As we shift into this belief, we experience a sense of relief, hope, and joy. We find ourselves giving others the benefit of the doubt and believing the best in people. As our thoughts toward the outer world shift, we radiate joy, magnetizing others to us—attracting true, deep friendships, as well as more influence and impact than ever before.

Not only do we experience uninhibited joy, but we become unstoppable: standing in our divine power, exceeding our wildest dreams, and living a life we wholly and completely love.

The bottom line is that *you* choose the meaning you will give to an event. *You* choose how the event will make you feel. You may automatically choose one meaning but then find yourself feeling stuck or sucked into a downward spiral of painful emotions. When you notice this and are ready to feel better, you can shift the meaning that you've given that event to something that better serves you.

When you choose to believe that life is happening for you, you open yourself up to a world of joy, love, and deep connections.

Who am I to tell you this is possible? I am a licensed therapist and have been a certified trauma therapist. I am the founder and owner of multimillion-dollar mental health counseling centers with dozens of incredible team members serving hundreds of clients each week. And most importantly, I am someone who gets to experience deep, authentic joy daily as I have chosen to live life with this belief in the forefront.

Let me give you a few examples of how choosing to believe that life is happening for me has played out in my life. In a simple day-to-day example, when I am trying to get somewhere in a hurry and I encounter a red light, I am grateful for it as I think maybe it's preventing me from getting in an accident farther up the road, or perhaps at the time I will now arrive, the perfect parking spot will be opening up. In another simple example, I arrived at the airport the other day to find that my flight was delayed by over three hours. I was annoyed for a minute, but then as I shifted to remembering that life is happening for me, I realized I would now have several uninterrupted hours to read my book.

In October 2019, I was T-boned as I was proceeding through a green light. My car spun, causing a concussion and, subsequently, post-concussion syndrome with post-concussive migraines. I was not able to work at all (or look at any screens) for several months, and then in a very limited capacity as I healed over the next few years. And three years later, I am still not fully healed. Many people would feel this was extremely unfair and remain stuck in anger and despair. However, within the first few days, I realized that this was an opportunity for me to rest, to stop being so busy and to just be; I couldn't do anything else anyway, so I may as well do my best to enjoy this time I was given! After several months, I hired someone to run my businesses because I was not able to do it. As I healed, I realized what a blessing this was, as it gave me the time and space to travel more, to spend more time with my loved ones, and to bring this message into the world. I have been able to clearly see how my accident was life happening for me, but it is not always so clear.

In March 2020, a paternal aunt I was extremely close to died. A week and a half later, a maternal uncle passed away. And a couple months later, a paternal aunt died. Then at the beginning of July, a cousin who was like a brother to me died very unexpectedly. And the next month, my twelve-year-old dog passed away.

This was a lot of loss in a short time. I am not able to clearly see how these deaths are life happening for me, but I choose to believe they are. I choose to believe they are because it fills me with hope amid the sadness. I still feel sad. I still feel these losses, but I choose not to be consumed by them. I choose not to stay stuck in these feelings so I can continue to live the way I know they all would have wanted.

Another way to think about this concept of life happening for us is through what Dr. Sue Morter calls the "bus stop conversation." Imagine several souls are at the bus stop waiting for the bus to bring them to earth for this life. They are sharing with each other what they want to learn and at what level, on a scale of one to ten, they want to learn it. One soul says, "I want to learn forgiveness at a level ten," and another says, "I want to learn self-compassion at a level ten." A third soul asks the first, "What circumstance might you need to learn forgiveness at a level ten?" The first soul thinks for a while and then says, "I think a drunk driver would need to hit my family's car and kill all of my family members for me to truly learn how to forgive at a level ten." And then looking around adds, "Who will volunteer to do this for me so that I can learn forgiveness at a level ten?" It's quiet for a while, then the second soul says, "I will. I want to learn self-compassion at a level ten, and this will give me the opportunity to do it." And then they hop on the bus for this wild ride of life—consciously forgetting their pre-arranged agreement.

In choosing to adopt the "bus stop conversation" perspective, not only will you believe life is happening for you, but you will search out what you can learn and how you can grow from every challenging or traumatic experience that happens in your life. How might this change your life? What might you learn? How might you grow?

What if you choose to believe that life is happening for you—always, in all ways? What might be different for you? What emotions might you get to release, and what might you get to step into? How might this impact your relationships? How might this impact your business?

You get to choose the meaning you assign to every situation.

You can choose to believe that life is happening for you.

You can start today.

As you release the victim mentality in every facet of your life and choose to believe that life is happening for you, you will experience more joy than you ever thought possible. This is the steppingstone that allows you to release oppressive expectations and focus on love: loving yourself, your family, your team, your clients.

From this place of joy, your family and friends will get to experience more quality time with their grounded, joyful partner/parent/friend. Your team members will be lifted up and empowered, and you will see creativity and productivity soar. Your clients will feel your love and your joy and will want to know how else they can work with you, grow with you. New business opportunities and new friends/partners/clients will be magnetized to you, and your influence and impact will grow exponentially.

The time is now. Are you ready?

My invitation to you is to try this as an experiment: for one week, choose to believe that life is happening for you. See how you feel. See what shifts. I would love to hear about your results.

ABOUT LINDSAY SMITH, LCSW

Lindsay Smith is a leading authority in Having. It. All! Lindsay provides CEO coaching for successful female entrepreneurs who have poured everything into their business to the exclusion of the rest of their life and know it is time for a change. She supports them in continuing to grow their business, while elevating their relationships, loving themselves, and bringing the things they love back into their life, and experiencing deep, authentic joy daily.

Lindsay is also a licensed clinical social worker and the founder of Being Your Best Self. Lindsay's mission is to end unnecessary suffering by eradicating the victim mentality and creating abundant joy as individuals choose to believe that life is happening for them. Always. In all ways. From this new paradigm, individuals are easily able to embrace profound self-love and experience more joy than ever before in their health, wealth, and relationships.

Lindsay created Being Your Best Self, a personalized, self-paced, online course, to help achieve that mission. Being Your Best Self is available to both individuals and corporations. To find out more about Lindsay's coaching and programs, visit www.bestselfelite.com or email Lindsay at lindsay@bestselfelite.com.

Lindsay is also the founder of Teen Therapy Center of Silicon Valley (www.teentherapycentersv.com) and Family Therapy Center of Silicon Valley (www.familytherapycentersv.com). Lindsay created a game called Talk About It! to enhance communication between teens and adults through fun and familiar card and dice games with a twist. To learn more about how this game can support you and your teens or how to get this game, visit www.talkaboutitgames.com.

FINDING MY STRENGTH

Phellicia Sorsby

I fell in love with my seventh-grade sweetheart. I dated him throughout all my school years and married him at the age of seventeen in twelfth grade. As a very young woman, I became a wife. But not just a wife, a military wife. I was a mother of twin boys at the age of twenty-two and a mother of four sons by age twenty-eight. I supported my husband's military career very much, always putting country and family first.

I took great pride in being a mother and wife, and while taking care of them, sadly, I forgot to take care of myself also. Now don't get me wrong, I am very much in tune with the fact that I exist. But I just didn't make my needs a priority. Not like I did with my sons' and husband's needs.

By age thirty-seven, I was divorced with four sons to raise alone. I became the sole support for four other humans. I struggled to hold down a full-time job and often several part-time positions as well. This type of lifestyle can break the strongest of women but breaking is not in my makeup.

While married, my husband cheated on me twice, and by my choice I stayed. Now my decision to stay did not come without a price. The more I worked at being the best wife and mother, the more I seemed to be drowning. I forgave my husband the first time because I was raised in a two-parent household, as was my spouse. I fought to raise our sons in a household that had a mother and a father. I thought it was my duty to forgive him and stay. You know, as long as I was not being physically abused. I didn't give any thought to the mental or emotional abuse.

The second time, I forgave him because I didn't want the stigma and embarrassment of being divorced. Well, that didn't do me any good because my husband asked me for a divorce. He said he had fallen out of love with me. Go figure, who knew? So, one of the things that I thought made me—being a wife—was no longer part of me.

During the separation, I took the high road when things became difficult. I would work that much harder to rise above. While separated, we purchased a home. We had one built from the ground up. We would go to the development when my husband came to see the boys and bask in the progress. Now I must say, I still held onto hope of the possibility of keeping the family together. I felt my sons were owed that. I have always believed that children deserve the very best from both their parents. We ask to have them, not the other way round, so we as parents should give them the very best part of us. But that is not how things worked out, and I was left to raise four sons alone.

Becoming a single parent ranked right up there with being one of the most difficult things I ever had to do. I never set out to be an unmarried woman with children. I always said I would never have a child out of wedlock, that I wanted to be married when I had children. But there I was, a single mother with four sons to raise. I was so fearful that my sons would be lost without their father in their lives. I must say that fear became fuel to not fail them, which turned into me not failing myself. I had strength when I was married, but I never knew the depth of my strength until I became a single mother. I wanted the absolute best for my sons, and just because I was alone, that was not reason enough for them to have anything less. With intensity of wanting the best for myself and my sons, I pushed to make a life for us.

Was it hard? I would say that is an understatement. I was the mother, father, homemaker, taxi driver, teacher, student, cook, disciplinary, friend, and provider for five individuals.

As for motherhood, after my divorce, I really didn't see much of a change. When I was married, I was the planner, fixer, and doer of the marriage. So, without my husband, I continued to be and do those same things. The only difference was I took full credit for it. I no longer made it seem as if my husband had a say in it. When I was married, I would suggest things for the family to do, and ask what he thought only to receive the reply, "I don't care, do whatever you want." So, I continued with that path and took full credit for it. I no longer made it seem as if my husband had a say, because he didn't.

One of the first things I promised myself was that my sons' lives would not be stuck in one place because their parents were divorced. That they would not suffer due to being raised in a single-family household. So, I pushed that much harder to never be left behind or considered second or less than because of my status. Being a military spouse, I had moved quite a bit, so my grade status in the federal government was a low GS-5. Because that salary was not enough to live on, I worked part-time as a bank telemarketer and at WAWA as a deli attendant. I found the strength to do what was needed to live the lifestyle I believed my sons and I deserved. Although I had two years of college under by belt, promotions seem hard to attain. So, I decided to go back to college to earn my bachelor's. I graduate one week after my twin sons graduated from high school.

There were times that I was so tired, I didn't know which way was up. I can truly say that for the first part of my adult life, I was living for someone else. First, my husband and next my sons. At some point, I finally stopped and took a good look at where I fit in my priorities. I noticed that I wasn't even in the top five, and I knew something had to change.

I made some much-needed changes and took the steps to get to know myself. At first, I thought by doing this I would lose the good things I had accomplished. Like the love I feel and show my sons. But then I realized that love I felt and showed my sons was good because I made it so, and that was not going to change. I was a hands-on type of mother. I volunteered for team mom at the school. My sons were in extra curriculum activities that took up many evenings and often weekends. The boys always had a home-cooked meal. I would line two or three crock pots on the kitchen counter before I left for work, and while I was working, dinner was cooking for the night. Sundays were my time to do nothing, or things within in the house—as much as I could. Then we started all over again on Monday.

I believe as women, we are often fed to believe that we cannot make it. I see this in so many women. I was very blessed to have a very strong role model who was my mother instill in me that I could do anything if I put it in my mind to do just that. I have a saying when I am told *no*, I just turn it around to *on*. Because it's *on* with me to show you that it can be done. As a woman of color and single parent, I have been told *no* more than any one person should.

I believe we must carve out the path that is best for us. It may not be turning right when everyone else has turned right. You may need to take a sharp left, and that is okay. Your path is what you make with the strength you have, and you are stronger than you know. You must believe in yourself and always know that you are important to you. That is where it starts. It took me some years to remember that, and now that I have it, it will not let it go!

ABOUT PHELLICIA SORSBY

Most people go through life not knowing what their purpose is, searching for what and where they fit. I was fortunate to be a people person all my life. I believe my purpose on this earth is to be of service to others. I am the proud mother of four amazing sons, all successful in their own right. I am a very involved GiGi to nine of the most wonderful grandchildren anyone could ever have. Marriage and motherhood are two things that are very dear to me. I have not succeeded at marriage, but as for motherhood, I *am* a success. I am a very outgoing individual, and I never meet a stranger. I am also a caring and loving individual who sees the best in people even when they themselves don't. I feel that each of us are gifted with an inner strength, that if we allow ourselves permission to embrace that empowerment, we will find the inner peace.

I live and love life to the fullest, and I am here to support you. I want to help you be the very best version of yourself you can be.

I can be contacted at the following emails:

psbebes@gmail.com
ejjhbebes@verizon.net

STEP INTO YOUR LEGACY

Dr. Angela Sadler Williamson

In spring 2014, I was sitting in my graduation regalia at Music City Center in Nashville, Tennessee, eagerly awaiting the time I could officially say I was a graduate. Our commencement speaker was veteran political strategist Donna Brazile, the first African American to manage a presidential campaign. Throughout my educational journey, I have listened to countless commencement speakers, and to be honest, I can't remember their names or what they said. But this commencement address would be different for me.

In sharing her story with us at the podium that day, Ms. Brazile challenged us to take a risk by saying, "Don't be afraid to ask questions."

I was at the point in my life where Ms. Brazile's address was exactly what I needed to hear because it would be her advice that guided me when I finally stepped into my legacy.

Just one year after hearing Ms. Brazile's inspirational commencement address, I would understand the significance of stepping into your legacy and the clues leading to it as I traveled its winding road—I just needed to pay attention.

The first clue is that small steps lead to a lasting legacy.

Small Steps Lead to a Lasting Legacy

It's the small steps that lead to each monumental event in our journey.

Rosa Parks started taking small steps into her legacy by joining the NAACP and starting the NAACP Youth Council prior to her legendary decision on December 1, 1955. And for me, creating a video for my father-in-law's memorial service in March 2015 would be my small step. Little did I know that creating this video would change my life.

During this time, my father-in-law's two sisters stayed with us. One sister, Carolyn, was the personal caretaker and attendant for our cousin Rosa Parks. While she stayed with us, she would tell me stories about working with Cousin Rosie and the work she was doing to keep her legacy alive in the city of Detroit. She and her friends' efforts continued Cousin Rosie's passion for the community, and especially children.

Since Cousin Rosie's death in 2005, Aunt Carolyn has received many commendations for this community work, including an award from the City of Los Angeles. It was during my conversations with her that I first considered capturing the Williamson family's oral history.

When I created the memorial video celebrating my father-in-law's life using my love of telling stories through video production, I realized I should be telling another person's story—the true story of our cousin, Rosa Parks.

In April 2015, when I took the small step to move forward and produce this documentary, I made another discovery: a 2014 NAACP image award-winning book by Dr. Jeanne Theoharis titled, *The Rebellious Life of Mrs. Rosa Parks*. In this book, Dr. Theoharis provided new insight about our cousin Rosie and supported all the stories I'd heard about her over the years. Stories told by family members, not historians.

Our life story is made up of a series of small steps. It's a lesson I would continue to learn in my latest documentary, *Authentic*

Conversations: Deep Talk with the Masters, featuring motivational speakers Jack Canfield, Kate Butler, and Patty Aubery. In it, they share how each small step helped them achieve success in their lives.

Jack and Patty talk about their journey to build the billion-dollar brand *Chicken Soup for the Soul,* which included 146 rejections from publishers around the country before one publisher took a chance and published their first book. Kate talks about how facing a serious medical issue in her twenties allowed her to reevaluate life and start the path to the life she is living today.

Small steps build your legacy on a strong foundation, and without them, it could crumble. Without Jack and Patty's small steps, we wouldn't have *Chicken Soup for the Soul,* a book series that would go on to inspire millions of people across the world. Without the small steps of Kate Butler, women worldwide would never be able to fulfill their dreams of being international best-selling authors. Without Rosa Parks's small step of creating the NAACP Youth Council, the flyers for the Montgomery Bus Boycott wouldn't have made it to the masses. Lastly, without my small step to protect my family's legacy, we wouldn't have an Emmy-nominated documentary and the first feature documentary about Rosa Parks.

Taking small steps is just one part of creating a lasting legacy. Your legacy also needs a "support group" to help you move forward on your path.

A Tribe Strengthens Your Legacy

From her early days as secretary for the NAACP, Cousin Rosie knew that a tribe strengthens your legacy. Even before December 1, 1955, she was working with young people and encouraging them to fight for human rights. She would bring this same philosophy with her to Detroit and form bonds with her female cousins, like my Aunt Carolyn and her sisters.

The time spent by Cousin Rosie cultivating her tribe is why

her legacy is still alive and making changes in our society today. Toward the end of her life, Cousin Rosie would send Aunt Carolyn to represent her at events and even in movies.

Have you ever tried to accomplish a huge goal and just couldn't seem to make it happen? You could be missing your tribe to help guide you. Over the last fifteen years, I tried and failed to accomplish a big goal in my life—becoming a tenured professor. No matter what I tried, I could never seem to reach that goal.

Although I did have some amazing support, I realized that I didn't have a tribe to support me in this endeavor, and without it, I most likely would never achieve my goal. This was an important clue I was missing in trying to create this legacy. I'll admit it was very frustrating and disappointing *until* I examined the other parts of my life that *were* flourishing.

Before I started my documentary filmmaking journey, my tribe was forming. My friend, Trish Ollry, listened to me brainstorm about possibly doing a documentary about Rosa Parks and Aunt Carolyn. My friends Jenny Tate, Gina Uresti, Michelle Byers, Angela Cockrell, Denice Burkhardt, and Netta Green never stopped asking me about my documentary during the two-year production process. Most of these ladies would also attend the documentary premiere at the Culver City Film Festival in 2017.

My tribe would expand even further after I entered my first film festival. Three other filmmakers attended the Culver City Film Festival that year: Taryn Hough, Shana Gagnon, and Fiona Lincke. Taryn would be my lifeline for all things film festival and film-production related. Shana would give me tips on applying to film festivals and invite me to be co-community manager of "Women in Film—International," her Facebook group supporting women in film around the world. Fiona would not only freely share her expertise, but she and husband would also support me during a private screening of *My Life with Rosie* at the home of Roger Wolfson, a screenwriter and *Huffington Post* contributor.

The tribe I formed with *My Life with Rosie* guided me

through a part of my journey that was unknown territory. This tribe helped me gain confidence in my filmmaking skills and gave me the courage to keep applying to film festivals. As I continued stepping into my legacy, I would soon learn that a tribe can positively shift your entire focus for your greater purpose.

Authentic Conversations: Deep Talk with the Masters became a documentary in October 2021. It was a project I couldn't have completed without the help of producers Dave Judy and John Wright. Not only did they rearrange their lives in just twenty-four hours to meet me in Santa Barbara to shoot the interviews, but they also stayed on the documentary project and worked with me for two months straight so it would air on KLCS PBS on December 26, 2021.

But even with their tireless efforts, I needed more support to keep the project growing. That's when ten ladies stepped up to help me in January 2022: Denise McCormick, Angela Germano, Ellen Craine, Michelle Reinglass, Jodie Baudek, Angela Cockrell, and Denice Burkhardt from the *My Life with Rosie* tribe, and Jeanie Griffin, Laurel Joakimides, and Jan Sharpton Edwards came on board to help me take this documentary to the next level—live screenings.

Expanding my tribe with these ten ladies shifted the atmosphere in my journey. With their help, I was able to secure an original song for the documentary, start a nonprofit, raise funds for the re-edit, and be prepared for the documentary's first live screening in New Jersey. I learned so much about turning my vision into a viable business so I can continue to produce stories that uplift and motivate people to take action.

A tribe nurtures your legacy. If you are having issues moving forward, ask yourself, "Do I have a tribe?" A tribe gives you the positive energy to push onward, and without it, you may need to learn to pivot.

Pivoting Protects Your Legacy

LinkedIn contributors voted "pivot" as the word of the year in

2020. Although it became the new word to describe the act of adapting to doing business during the pandemic, it's not a new word to people actively creating their legacies. The ability is a necessity for avoiding becoming stagnant during your journey. The world would be a vastly different place if legacy makers didn't know when to pivot.

Imagine your husband sleeping with a gun because you're receiving death threats every day. Imagine suffering from ulcers because you are living in constant danger. Imagine being fired from your job for standing up for your beliefs and soon there-after, your husband loses his job just for being married to you. Finally, imagine your mother spending all night on the phone talking to her friend just to get the phone to stop ringing with death threats.

What the history books fail to mention was that in addition to being a victim of what today we'd call hate crime, Rosa Parks was also receiving hostility from the very organization she became the spokesperson for when she refused to give up her bus seat in 1955. The tension became so great that her mother began pressuring her to move to Detroit.

So, after thirty years of living in Montgomery, Alabama, Rosa Parks made the decision to move to Detroit in the summer of 1957. And with that move came the need to pivot—to form a new tribe that included her brother, nieces, nephews, and many cousins.

Soon after the Emancipation Proclamation was issued in 1863, the parents of Susan Mosely Grandison, a former slave, made a pivotal move to Mount Pleasant, Iowa, to provide educational opportunities for their children. In 1885, Susan became the first female African American graduate of Iowa Wesleyan University, and then three years later, the first African American to earn a master's degree from the university. Susan dedicated her life and career to ensuring that black students had the same opportunities to pursue a college degree that she had.

My choice to pivot my career goal of obtaining a tenured position in higher education was the hardest choice I've ever had to make. Cousin Rosie and Susan's parents' decisions to pivot wasn't an easy choice but a necessary one. Pivoting gives you the opportunity to uplift, empower, and motivate others to shape their own legacies.

If Cousin Rosie hadn't pivoted and moved to Detroit, Aunt Carolyn wouldn't have blossomed into a seasoned activist, who would then become my muse for *My Life with Rosie*. If Susan's family hadn't moved to Mount Pleasant, Iowa, the Susan Mosely Grandison Diversity and Inclusion Fund that supports the university's commitment to impacting change through education would never have come to be.

Learning to pivot during my career opened many doors, including being accepted into the Writers Guild of America West, featured in two #1 international best-selling books, a faculty fellowship at Fielding Graduate University, and hosting an interview show on PBS in Los Angeles.

As you follow the clues, you will have to step into your legacy even when others can't see it. And that takes faith.

Faith Moves Your Legacy Forward

Leaders of the Montgomery Improvement Organization didn't understand Rosa Parks's decision to leave Alabama and move to Detroit. They even questioned about how she could possibly continue activism in the North.

Although Cousin Rosie left Alabama for Detroit under a cloud of fear, she would only spend a moment there before realizing activism never sleeps. In February 1987, she co-founded a nonprofit organization specifically for the children of Detroit—the Rosa and Raymond Parks Institute for Self Development, on which my Aunt Carolyn served as a board member. Even into her nineties, Cousin Rosie actively motivated young people to protect our human rights—because she knew activism never sleeps.

When I started producing *My Life with Rosie* in my mid-forties,

I had a very small tribe. I remembered telling a former colleague about my new project and she looked at me like I was an alien. Even one of my cousins asked me if I was ever going to finish the documentary.

I admit it's hard to believe when we can't see it but stepping into your legacy means you must believe in it even when others don't. That is what faith is all about. It only takes a tiny amount of faith to move mountains.

Because of Cousin Rosie's faith in her activism, she continued most of her work in the city of Detroit until her death in October 2005. During her time in Detroit, she received some of our country's greatest honors, including the Presidential Medal of Freedom in 1996 and the Congressional Gold Medal in 1999. Rosa Parks's statue in the National Statuary Hall of the United States Capitol is the only statue in the hall not linked with a state, and the first full-length statue of an African American in the Capitol.

I finished *My Life with Rosie,* and my former colleague's university invited me to speak and screen my documentary on campus. My cousin became my biggest cheerleader during my two-year film festival run.

Your legacy needs you to have faith in your journey so that it can grow and reach others with your message. Cousin Rosie, and then Aunt Carolyn, kept their faith even when they experienced hardships. Both were powerful community activists even when they did not have jobs because roadblocks strengthen your legacy.

Roadblocks Strengthen Your Legacy

The most inspiring story in *My Life with Rosie* is when Aunt Carolyn tells the story of how she moved into Cousin Rosie's legacy of activism when she was laid off from General Motors. Her choice to work in her community even while laid-off is what helped her start Community United for Progress.

Now here's what's so interesting about Community United for Progress. Remember earlier in this chapter where I mentioned a private screening of *My Life with Rosie* at Roger Wolfson's home? After I screened the documentary, a civil rights attorney introduced herself to me and told me she had been donating to Community United for Progress for years and did not know that it was started in Detroit by my aunt and her friends. The civil rights attorney was so excited to find out how this organization started.

Everybody with Angela Williamson has been airing on KLCS PBS since September 2020, and everyone always asks me how I got an interview show on television. To be honest, the show found me through legendary voice-over artist, Bill Rogers. Starting a new show during a pandemic was a challenge, which introduced many roadblocks, including losing access to our studio for ten months. Even without a studio, KLCS PBS stayed committed to the show, and we completed season one. We're currently in season four with the hopes of going national, and we now have our first sponsor. Thank you, Fireheart Pictures!

Aunt Carolyn learned from Cousin Rosie that roadblocks strengthen our stories. I remembered these stories as we faced challenges in the first season of *Everybody with Angela Williamson*. Roadblocks are part of our journey. I want to challenge you to not get discouraged and never forget you are worthy.

You Are Worthy!

There are times in our lives when we feel overwhelmed by our circumstances and we start to feel unworthy. You are not alone. When this happens, someone will come into your life to remind you of your worthiness. This happened to me in March 2019 during my first trip to Iowa.

As the 2019 *Belle Babb Mansfield Award* recipient, I participated in a student-led panel discussion. One of the student moderators told me that her participation on the panel was the highlight of her college career. Her enthusiastic comments allowed me to replay the moments of my amazing journey with *My Life with Rosie,* and I realized how this documentary was making a positive impact in people's lives.

The following day, a lovely woman came up to me and told me how much I encouraged her, and she gave me a card and a book titled *Women Who Impact*. She suggested that my story be in her publisher's next book, *Women Who Illuminate*.

During your lowest point, people will appear to remind you that you are worthy! As I finish this legacy roadmap, I want to remind you to always be gracious on your legacy journey.

Be Gracious on Your Legacy Journey

When you're humble, you'll naturally be courteous, kind, and pleasant to others. Donna Brazile's advice to ask questions was her way of reminding us to remain humble. But she's not the only person to give us this lesson.

One of my favorite photos from our wedding doesn't even feature us. It's a photo of Rosa Parks standing on the balcony at our wedding venue smiling down at our bridal party. In fact, my husband and I had already walked inside the venue before we realized we were walking by ourselves. We walked back outside to see the entire wedding party looking up in awe with a smiling Rosa Parks waving to them. You see, Rosa Parks didn't tell our bridal party to stop and look up; her mere presence, the grace she spent her entire life showing us during her darkest hours, is what stopped our wedding party.

Rosa Parks was the epitome of grace and showed us how to step into our legacy. She stayed graceful when she was leading youth to fight for human rights. She stayed graceful when she was afraid to sleep in her home because of death threats. She stayed graceful when she couldn't get another job well after the bus boycott ended and had to move hundreds of miles away so she and her family could survive. Cousin Rosie stayed graceful and inspired others until the very end. As she would say: "Freedom fighters never retire."

But let's keep it real. We all know the best advice always comes from mom. From when I was very young, my mother would tell me to be graceful in every interaction with others because I could be entertaining angels on assignment without even knowing it.

These legacy trailblazers: Cousin Rosie, Aunt Carolyn, Donna Brazile, Susan Mosely Grandison, and many others are our past and present angels leaving us clues for creating a long-lasting legacy. Most importantly, they inspire us to be authentic as we take a stand against racism, discrimination, social injustice, and gender inequality, because our world needs legacy makers now more than ever to help us heal and move forward.

Now, go step into your legacy!

[Dr. Williamson delivered this story as the commencement address at Iowa Wesleyan University's 2022 Commencement Ceremony on April 30, 2022.]

ABOUT DR. ANGELA SADLER WILLIAMSON

Dr. Angela Sadler Williamson is a #1 international best-selling author, Emmy-nominated filmmaker, multiple Telly awards recipient, and former producer and copywriter for major broadcast TV and cable news networks. Her Emmy-nominated documentary *My Life with Rosie* is about the activism of her cousin Rosa Parks. It has won numerous "Best Documentary" titles at film festivals across the country.

Her international best-selling companion book *My Life with Rosie: A Bond Between Cousins* has been named "Best Children's Book about Black History." She recently released her second documentary, *Authentic Conversations: Deep Talk with the Masters* featuring Jack Canfield, Patty Aubery, and Kate Butler.

She is also the host of weekly interview show *Everybody with Angela Williamson*, which discusses diversity within education, the arts, and people. As a dedicated philanthropist proudly carrying on her cousin's legacy, she harnesses the power of her twenty-five-plus years of experience in education and media for social good through her involvement in projects and organizations that focus on improving the communities they serve.

Connect with Dr. Williamson:

www.drangelasadlerwilliamson.com

Have you ever dreamed of
becoming a published author?
Do you have a story to share?
Would the world benefit
from hearing your message?

Then we want to connect with you!

The *Inspired Impact Book Series* is looking to connect with
women who desire to share their stories with the goal of
inspiring others.

We want to hear your story!

Visit www.katebutlerbooks.com to learn more
about becoming a Featured Author in the #1 International
Best-selling *Inspired Impact Book Series.*

Everyone has a story to share!
Is it your time to create your legacy?

May your soul be uplifted and the words of these pages inspire you to continue to lead with your infinite divine light to your fullest expression in leaving your legacy!

Authors of Leading with Legacy

REPRINTED WITH PERMISSIONS

Kate Butler, CPSC
Rosalyn Baxter-Jones, MD, MBA
Dr. Lucette Beall
Shalini Saxena Breault
Donna Nudel Brown
Ellen M. Craine
Ann Marie Esparza-Smith M.A.
Claudia Fernandez-Niedzielski
Angela Germano
Jeanie Griffin
Laurel Joakimides
Tara LePera
Denise McCormick, M.A.E.
Kristi Ann Pawlowski
Michelle A. Reinglass
Lisa Marie Runfola
Samantha Ruth
Lindsay Smith, LCSW
Phellicia Sorsby
Dr. Angela Sadler Williamson